MEMOIRS
—— OF A ——
PSYCH NURSE
AND OTHER STORIES

MEMOIRS OF A PSYCH NURSE

AND OTHER STORIES

SUE MITZEL TOURTELOT

Copyright © 2012 by Sue Mitzel Tourtelot.

Library of Congress Control Number: 2012917607
ISBN: Softcover   978-1-4797-2118-4
          Ebook   978-1-4797-2119-1

All rights reserved. No part of this book may be reproduced or transmitted in any form or by any means, electronic or mechanical, including photocopying, recording, or by any information storage and retrieval system, without permission in writing from the copyright owner.

This book was printed in the United States of America.

To order additional copies of this book, contact:
Xlibris Corporation
1-888-795-4274
www.Xlibris.com
Orders@Xlibris.com
120199

TABLE OF CONTENTS

1. SUE WHO? 1
2. SURGERY ROTATION 6
3. FIRST JOB 9
4. TUNE IN TOMORROW 13
5. DR. JAMES, COME QUICK 15
6. WHO'S GUARDING THE KNIVES? 18
7. A WEEK ON EAST TWO 21
8. MARIA'S STORY 24
9. FLYING HIGH 28
10. GLUE DOESN'T ALWAYS HOLD THINGS TOGETHER 31
11. MR. McDUGGIN DID WHAT? 33
12. A NURSE'S DILEMMA 36
13. WHAT COULD I HAVE BEEN DOING? 38
14. WAS SHE A DISILLUSIONED MISTRESS OR JUST AN ANGRY WOMAN? 40
15. THE ECLIPSE OF MY HEART 42
16. CHRISTMAS MEMORIES 47

17. WHO'S STEALING THE NARCOTIC'S..50

18. FOUR EMPTY BEDS..53

19. WHO KILLED MR. MYERS?..57

20. THEY JUST WANTED TO BE BLOOD BROTHERS.....................59

21. HE'S MINE?...61

22. DOES COWBOY STILL HUNT BUFFALO.....................................64

23. NO FEELING..66

24. WHO'LL SEE DR. EDIE?..68

25. HOLIDAY TEA...70

26. HOW DID HE KNOW?...73

27. RON'S STORY..76

28. SINS OF THE FATHERS...82

29. EVENTUALLY YOU HAVE TO PAY THE PIPER........................86

30. BABIES HAVING BABIES..89

31. WALKING THE DOGS...93

32. DR. B IS BACK...97

DEDICATION

July 27, 1943—January 9, 1967

    I am dedicating this book to my loving husband, Lonny L. Mitzel, who was killed in Vietnam on January 9, 1967. He always encouraged me in my work with adolescents in a psychiatric setting. He wanted to become a psychologist after his time in the Air Force. I miss him every day.

ACKNOWLEDGMENTS

I want to thank the hundreds of patients and clients, who have shared their lives with me. They taught me so very much. Some of their stories are sad, and some are funny. All the stories are true and made an impact on my life.

In particular, I want to thank four women who so generously read my stories and edited them. First, Jane Kopp, who started a writing class in her home and gave me so much encouragement. Also, Judy Slavens, Charlotte Ridley and Andrea Antico who so generously corrected my grammatical errors.

ABOUT THE AUTHOR

As a nurse since 1962, I never got bored due to the many nursing opportunities available to me. I've worked on medical units, In and Outpatient psychiatric settings, a doctor's office, a nursing home and taught a Medication Administration course for the State Health Department.

My favorite specialties were psychiatric and community health nursing.

I especially liked working with adolescents in a psychiatric setting.

I started with a Diploma from Bryn Mawr Hospital School of Nursing. Sixteen years later I received a Bachelor's Degree from Metro State College, and three years later a Master's Degree in Community Health Nursing from the University of Colorado Health Sciences Center.

I learned so much and I am so grateful to the hundreds of clients who helped to make me the nurse I am today.

SUE WHO?

We were destined to meet. After all, we had been mixed up in the hospital seventy-one years ago, this month. I was born on August 9, 1941, weighing five pounds and four ounces, to George and Bessie Fritz. When I was four hours old, I turned blue and was put into an incubator to get more oxygen. Mother and I stayed in the hospital for the next nine days. On August 14, 1941, Sue Ann was born to Daisy and Lincoln Fitz. Sue Ann weighed nine pounds and eight ounces.

Imagine my mother's surprise on August 15th when the nurse walked into her room saying, "Here's your daughter, Mrs. Fritz." My mother took one look at the chubby, red faced, curly, dark haired baby and yelled, "That's not my baby. My baby is little." The embarrassed nurse took the baby and hurried out of her room. Ten minutes later, she returned with me saying, "Now I know why you said the first baby wasn't your little girl."

The next day when I was out of danger, my dad brought a dozen red roses for my mother. He stopped at the nurses' station and said, "Could you put these in a vase for my wife?" My mother never got the roses. I wonder if Daisy got the roses and how she explained them to Lincoln.

My mother became wheelchair-bound with rheumatoid arthritis when I was very young. My dad spent all the more time with me trying to be both a mother and a father. Since I was very active in team sports, my dad coached all of my athletic teams. In eighth grade, I played basketball for my church team. The league was at the local YWCA. Sue Ann played in the same league for Mt. Roes Junior High School. At that time, women's basketball was played with the forwards on one half of the court and guards on the other half.

You guessed it. I played forward and Sue Ann was my guard. Both teams had three wins and no loses the night we became opponents, Sue Ann was about two inches shorter than I was, a little heavier and very intimidating. At half-time, the score was tied and my dad said, "If you girls pass the ball more and look for the open person, you can win this game." Then he looked over at me and saw me taking off my sneakers.

"What are you doing?" he asked.

"I'm not playing any more. That girl guarding me said she'd beat the crap out of me if I make anymore points." The rest of the team looked from me to my dad wondering what was going to happen.

"Susan, put your shoes back on. No one gets beat up over a simple basketball game."

The second half started and my guard continued to elbow, trip and verbally intimate me. I got mad and started throwing elbows too. At the end of the third quarter the score was Mt. Rose 17 and St. Matthews 16. My dad said we were communicating well and we should just to keep up the good work. My guard had four fouls. Maybe with luck, she'd get another one and foul out.

My team really came on strong during the last quarter. Our guards didn't allow our opponents more than seven shots at the basket and our forwards were all scoring. The final score was St. Matthews 25, Mt. Rose 22. After the last whistle blew, my guard grabbed my arm and said, "I'll see you in the dressing room." I didn't go back into the dressing room. My friend, Pat, brought my jeans and sweatshirt out to me.

There were ten teams in the league that year and St. Matthews finished in second place with Mt. Rose finishing third.

One year and ten months later, I started high school. William Penn Senior High had a student body of twenty-four hundred with eight hundred and fifty students in the sophomore class. That one high school took students from seven junior high schools.

I walked into my new home room with great trepidation. In ninth grade, I felt all powerful and able to deal with any situation but, remembering the hard time I had in seventh grade, I was scared. I only recognized four other girls from my junior high school.

Miss Jones, my home room teacher, was a portly, round faced, friendly looking lady. She asked us all to stand around the perimeter of the room so she could seat us alphabetically.

When Miss Jones said, "Behind Beth Bowers is Sue Ann Fitz," I thought she really messed up my name. I stood forward and said, "It's Susan Fritz."

Just then my basketball nemesis walked up, and glaring at me, said "Oh no it isn't, it's Sue Ann Fitz and don't you forget it."

Still in shock, I quietly took my seat behind Bonnie Fox, who sat behind Sue Ann Fitz. Susan Garvin was seated directly behind me. I could hardly wait until lunch to tell my friends who was in my home room.

At that time, students did not get to choose their classes so, Susan, Sue Ann and Susan would spend the next few years in the same college preparatory classes.

Sue Ann and I shared an interest in team sports and played on several intramural teams together. This eventually led, in spite of our unpromising beginning between Sue Ann Fitz and me, to a long lasting friendship.

At the end of tenth grade my parents told me that they didn't have the money to send me to college. I would have to switch over to the business track for my junior and senior year. I was devastated. All I ever wanted was to teach physical education.

To receive enough credits to switch to the business track, I had to take four hours of typing during summer school. That was the first summer I would not be able to attend church camp. I had dreamed of becoming a camp counselor, but with two months of summer school, camp was out.

Since my mother was crippled, I was responsible for most of the house work.

Monday was wash day, Tuesday a free day, Wednesday ironing day, Friday clean the whole apartment and Saturday go to market with Dad. When would I ever find time for summer school?

I went to summer school from 8:00 a.m. till noon Monday thru Friday for eight weeks. The first two hours, I was with students who, like me were taking typing for the first time. I did fairly well. From 10:00 a.m. till noon, I was with students who had flunked typing and were repeating the course. They typed much faster and made me extremely nervous. Until that class, I had never sat still more then an hour. I thought I would go crazy.

Only one time in two months did I type twenty-five words a minute with only one error. It was no shock to me when Mr. DeBerti called me up to his desk the last day of class. He said, "Susan, you have failed this class. If you promise never to take typing again as long as you are in this school district, I'll give you a D instead of an F."

"I promise," I said, and then cried the whole way home. Now what was I going to do? What were my parents going to say? I was still crying when I walked in the back door. Throwing myself onto my Dad's wooden rocking chair, I wailed, "Mom, what am I going to do? I flunked the typing class! He gave me a D, but I had to promise not to take typing again. I just got so nervous I couldn't type without looking at my fingers."

With a tear rolling down her cheek, my mother said, "It's okay, Susan we'll just have to figure out something else for you to do. You worked really hard this summer."

September came, and I was back on the college prep track with my friends.

My best friend from church, Penny, was a year ahead of me in school. She went off to nursing school when she graduated. Sue Ann and Helen, another friend, joined The Future Nurses, of America Club. I didn't. Penny came home from nursing school about once a month. She regaled me with stories about her classes, her patients and, most of all, her independence. As I watched two of my friends apply to nursing schools, that became a viable option for me.

My grandmother gave a gift of five-hundred dollars to each grand child who went on to higher education after high school. My first year of nursing school cost three-hundred and fifty dollars, the second year one-hundred dollars and the third year fifty dollars. My grandmother made it possible for me to go to nursing school.

I applied to three hospital based schools but I really wanted to go to Bryn Mawr Hospital School of Nursing.

Sue Ann and I both applied to Bryn Mawr. Sue Ann was a straight A student with an emphasis on hard sciences. I, on the other hand, was a straight B student who excelled in gym class. We both got accepted at Bryn Mawr, and I was always convinced that my high school sent Sue Ann's transcripts instead of mine.

In February of our senior year, Sue Ann and I headed to Bryn Mawr for a day-long physical exam. First, we walked through a tub of water and then onto paper so a podiatrist could see if we had flat feet, which, of course I had. Next, an orthopedist checked our backs. Back injuries are very common if proper lifting techniques are not used. Sue Ann went off to talk with Dr. Jones while I was examined by a medical doctor. After lunch, we switched and I went to see Dr. Jones. When we met up again I asked Sue Ann, "What kind of doctor is Dr. Jones?"

"A psychiatrist," she said. "Why, what did you say to him?"

"Well, he kept pulling on his beard and asked me to tell him about my family." I told him I had a mom who was crippled, a dad who worked in a factory, and a married sister. He asked what my hobbies were and I said dinosaurs and ice skating. You don't think he'll think I'm crazy, do you?"

Sue Ann said, "I don't know. What else did you tell him?"

"I told him that I'm good with my hands whether it's putting models together or playing basketball." Then, he said I could leave. When I got to to the door, I couldn't get it open. I almost started to cry and he said, "Just turn the knob to the left." I did and it opened. I know he's going to think I'm weird but he is, too.

Sue Ann and I were both accepted at Bryn Mawr. I was really glad that I was going to Bryn Mawr because they had a good basketball team and we could play more basketball together. Too this day, Sue Ann and I are close friends.

SURGERY ROTATION

The big day finally came. Yesterday, we started our four-week surgery rotation. We learned the proper procedures for washing our hands and arms for five minutes, putting on a gown, cap, mask and sterile gloves. Today, we would observe our first surgery.

Dr. Hendrickson was going to remove an abdominal hernia from a fifty-year old woman. The six of us were wide-eyed and anxious, standing across the table from him. He started out by telling us how she got the hernia and what he was going to do to correct it. With a sterile sponge, he scrubbed her abdomen with a strong antibacterial soap, then using a very sharp scalpel, he made a six-inch cut beside her umbilicus. Initially, the area became very white and then turned red with blood.

All of a sudden, Debra, one of my classmates, fainted and fell onto the patient's abdomen. As Dr. Hendrickson swore about student nurses and their blunders, Miss Miller, our clinical instructor, dragged Debra out of the operating room. As you might have expected, Dr. Hendrickson had to re-gown, re-glove, re-drape and re-scrub the patient. He was furious. He spent the next fifteen minutes ranting and raving about allowing student nurses to assist surgeons during surgery. As students, we had heard that surgeons were temperamental and high strung and now we were seeing it first hand.

We were required to choose a patient and write a case study report in each specialty. My surgery case study was Mr. Snyder. He had thyroid cancer and was going to have his thyroid gland removed. I met him and his wife the day before surgery. I would assist his surgeon during surgery and then follow him through his hospital stay and recovery. Fortunately for me, Dr. Hendrickson was not Mr. Snyder's surgeon.

After Debra's episode, I was nervous assisting in Mr. Snyder's thyroidectomy.

I didn't need to be because Mr. Snyder's surgeon and the surgical resident were very kind and explained each step to me. The surgery was going well, the thyroid gland was removed and the surgeon asked the resident if he wanted to close the surgical site. The surgeon told the anesthesiologist to start letting up on the anesthesia and started to leave the room. As soon as the anesthesia was let up, Mr. Snyder sat upright. Everyone started to yell at him to lie down. I was standing by the arm that had the intravenous anesthesia in it and was told to hold it down so it would not infiltrate if he bent his arm. I remember holding his arm above his elbow and at his wrist and being lifted right off the floor as he bent his arm. The anesthesiologist finally got him sedated again and the resident finished sewing up his neck.

Fifteen minutes later, I walked into the classroom in shock. I guess I was pale because my instructor asked me if I was okay. "He sat up before the operation was over," I said. I still couldn't believe what had just happened.

After class each day, I went to Mr. Snyder's room and sat with him. When he dosed off, I studied. The day before Mr. Snyder was discharged his surgeon came to see him. When his surgeon asked if he had questions he replied, "Doc, I had the strangest dream during surgery. I dreamed that I sat up before the operation was over and everyone was yelling at me to lie back down." With that, I held my notebook in front of my face so Mr. Snyder couldn't see me. I didn't know how the surgeon would reply and knew the expression on my face would tell Mr. Snyder the answer. The surgeon assured Mr. Snyder that it wasn't a dream and explained to him that because the thyroid tumor had speeded him up so much he woke up faster then expected. The Snyders' were very kind to me and because I had to work the following Christmas Day, they invited me to dinner after my shift.

Debra was not allowed to assist in any major surgeries after fainting that first day. She was relegated to assisting with wart removals. Guess what? The last week of our rotation she was to assist Dr. Hendrickson with the removal of a wart from a patient's neck.

While Rosemary and I were scrubbing for our next surgery, Debra was in Room One talking to the patient and preparing the surgical tray. In those days, you had to put the blade onto the scalpel and break a glass vial with the suture material in it. We were almost finished our five-minute scrub when we heard Debra calling us. "Rosemary, Sue, please come in here and help me."

"No way, Debra, we're not going to break scrub now, our arms are too sore already."

"Please come in, I think I'm bleeding." With that we both ran into Room One. Debra had dropped the scalpel after she had put the blade on it and it went into her leather shoe, cutting her big toe. While we were removing Debra's shoe, Dr. Hendrickson arrived. I can't repeat what he said while he sewed up her toe before removing the wart from the patient's neck. Debra was a straight A student in theory, but, practically, she had a ways to go.

FIRST JOB

Today was my second day as a graduate nurse, and I had no idea how much I would be learning in the following ten months. Since I was in my orientation period, I was not assigned a patient load. The head nurse told me to walk around and observe the two nurses passing medications and doing specific treatments.

I was walking down the south wing when a nurse aide came running out of Room 360 yelling, "Nurse come quick, the lady in Bed 2 is having a seizure." I ran into the room, and, sure enough, the lady was having a grand mal seizure. I tore apart her nightstand looking for a padded tongue blade or a toothbrush to hold down her tongue. There was none, so I leaped over the lady in Bed I and tore into her nightstand. I finally found a toothbrush, and, by the time I got over to the patient, the seizure was over and she was breathing quietly. Boy, did I ever feel foolish. I composed myself and walked out to the nurses' station to report to the head nurse. That was just the beginning.

The very next day, I was making rounds with an intern and his pager went off. He asked me to go to the phone and pick up his message. I looked at the name on his lab coat and left the room. At the nurse's station I asked how to pick up messages. The ward clerk told me and I called the operator. "I need to pick up Dr. Hogwot's message," I told the operator. "We don't have a doctor by that name." she said. I asked her what physicians were being paged and settled on a Dr. Howitt.

I took down the message, and when I turned around the head nurse and ward clerk were laughing so hard they were holding their stomachs. I turned beet red and walked down the hall to find Dr. Howitt. The physician's name was spelled Houghwout and that's why I thought it was pronounced Hogwot. I was quickly making a name for myself.

9

About three months later we received a frail, mute, paranoid looking, older female who had stopped eating and was trying to starve herself to death. The only room we had left was a private one at the far end of the hall. We put her in the room with plans to move her closer to the nurses' station as soon as we had a discharge. Her wrists were restrained so she wouldn't run away or harm herself.

Lunch came and there were just two of us passing out trays. The assistant head nurse, Linda, took the new patient's tray into her room and attempted to feed her. The lady remained mute, closed her mouth, and turned her head away. We still had a lot of trays to pass out, so Linda cut up her food and loosened one wrist, hoping she would eat something off the tray while we passed out the rest of the trays.

About ten minutes later, there was an overhead call for all available physicians to report to the emergency-room entrance. When we heard that call, Linda ran to the new patient's room because it was three stories above the emergency room. There, she found an empty bed with a set of cloth restraints still attached to the bedrails. The window, which would only open six inches, was open, and the curtain was blowing in the breeze. You guessed right. Our new patient had jumped out the window and landed in front of the ER entrance.

Ironically, she did not kill herself. She had a broken pelvis, left arm and left leg. She went immediately to the operating room and then to a surgical floor where she had a full time sitter. Unfortunately, our general hospital did not have a psychiatric unit, and we were not prepared to handle psychiatric patients on a medical unit.

Later that afternoon, an intern came to our unit and told us that he'd been one floor below us on the pediatric unit at lunchtime. He said a little boy came running out of his room and tugging on his lab coat yelled "Doctor, come quick, a lady just flew past my window." Five minutes later, the intern was surprised because a woman had indeed just flown past the little guy's window.

3C was a very busy unit and we were often understaffed. One evening, there were just two RN's and three nurse aides caring for forty patients. I was responsible for all the medications and intravenous fluids. It was imperative that an IV not run dry, but that's exactly what happened. The IV of Mr. Johnson, in room 361 Bed 2, had run out, and there was air halfway down the tubing. I was mortified. I turned the IV completely off and ran to call the intern on duty. He told me there wasn't more than 1 or 2 teaspoonfuls of fluid in the entire tubing and that was not enough to harm Mr. Johnson. I was told to remove the IV. I was sure I was giving Mr. Johnson an air embolism and would be responsible for his death. I checked on Mr. Johnson every fifteen minutes, for the rest of my shift. Before going home, I went into the dirty utility room and with a syringe measured how much fluid was in the entire IV tubing.

Because we were short staffed, I had to double back and work the day shift the next day. When I arrived on 3C, I went directly to room 361. There was only one bed in the room, and in it was Mr. Johnson's roommate. I got nauseated, weak and almost fainted. I ran to the nurses' station, yelling, "Where's Mr. Johnson?"

"He's down the hall in room 320. His roommate was snoring so loudly that he couldn't sleep, so we moved him," the night nurse said nonchalantly. I can't tell you how relieved I was, and what an impact that incident had on my career. That's probably the day my hair started to turn gray.

What a year that was! I met another young nurse and she was moving to Denver. I decided to be a pioneer and move there too. We applied for our temporary Colorado licenses and just waited.

Having graduated from a hospital on the "mainline" and not the one I was working in, I admit to having a chip on my shoulder. That chip was made larger by an orderly who had lived in a town on the mainline and as we walked our stroke patients, he fed my ego. He kept saying I was running circles around the other nurses and I bought it. Unfortunately, that led to trouble for me.

My head nurse loved me but to the day supervisor, who made out the schedules, didn't like my chip. One of my long time friends was getting married and asked me to participate in her wedding in a minor way. We got every third weekend off, and that would have been my weekend off, but to make sure, I requested it off. Mrs. Strayer, the day supervisor, scheduled me to work the 3:00p.m. to 11:00p.m. shift that Saturday. The wedding was at 2:00pm. Linda offered to work a split shift with me. She said I should work from 7:00am until 11:00a.m. and she would come in and work from 11:00a.m. until 7:00p.m. when I returned. What a wonderful idea. She said she'd leave a note for Mrs. Strayer. The following day, Mrs. Strayer called Linda into her office and said she would not okay the split shift and that I needed to work from 3:00p.m. to 11:00p.m. that day.

My evening supervisor suggested that I should call in sick for that shift if the day supervisor was going to be so rigid. Four days before the wedding, Mrs. Strayer called me into her office. She said she'd heard that I was going to call in sick on saturday. I told her that I hadn't made up my mind yet but was thinking about it.

She then said, "Susan, you're trying to get a temporary license to work in Colorado, aren't you?"

"Yes," I said.

"Well, if you call in sick on Saturday, I'll make sure you won't get that license."

Needless to say, I worked the 3:00p.m. to 11:00p.m. shift that Saturday and missed my friend's wedding. The following Monday I received my temporary license from Colorado. I was furious. Since I was a new graduate, I didn't know that Mrs. Strayer had no say in whether I got a temporary license in another state. I resigned and left the hospital two weeks later never to look back, but much wiser.

TUNE IN TOMORROW

"Tune in tomorrow and find out. Will Mary Ann Cunningham live through her kidney transplant?"

In 1964, I worked as a staff nurse on the women's medical unit of a large university hospital. It was there that I met Mary Ann. At twenty years of age, Mary Ann had had chronic kidney disease almost since birth. She had been on a list for a kidney transplant for three years. The best match is almost always a family member. In Mary Ann's case, her father was dead and her mother and sister were not a match so she was waiting for a miracle. In those days, university hospitals did not have transplant units. Patients went to a medical unit to be prepared for the transplant and then to a surgical floor after the transplant.

Mary Ann was receiving dialysis three times a week but that was not enough.

If she didn't receive a kidney soon, she would die. While awaiting a donor, Mary Ann was given large doses of steroids to prepare for a transplant. Since her kidneys weren't functioning, her doctors were limiting her fluid intake so severely that at times she would attempt to suck water from her washcloth and the plants in her room.

At one point, her output of urine was less then one ounce in an eight-hour period. None of the medicines were helping her to produce urine, so, out of frustration, her doctor asked her what she thought would help her. "Get me a beer," she stated. After finding out her favorite beer, the physician sent a medical student out for a beer. We all know that tea and beer are natural diuretics, but believe me, beer works the best. Mary Ann drank her beer and put out over a pint of urine in the next eight hours. That was cause for celebration by the nursing staff.

It was so difficult for us to watch Mary Ann beg for water. I can't imagine not being able to drink fluids when I get thirsty. Her skin became so dry and flaky and her hair so brittle that it would brake off when she combed her hair.

Finally, a donor was found and her steroids were increased. The steroids made her retain fluids, her hands and face became swollen and she became psychotic. The night before her surgery, I walked into her room and found her mother holding her down in the bed. Mary Ann was yelling, "Tune in tomorrow and find out if Mary Ann lived through her transplant." I talked calmly to Mary Ann and settled her down. Then, I put my arms around her mother and let her cry on my shoulder. She cried like her heart was broken; she had never seen Mary Ann act this way. I explained to her that the increase in steroids and the buildup of uremia caused her to behave this way.

The next morning after preparing her for surgery, I watched her go off to the operating room and said a prayer for her. She would wake up on the surgical floor.

I visited Mary Ann often on the surgical floor, and soon she was discharged from the hospital. She was still puffy from the steroids and anti-rejection drugs but her kidney was working well. Mary Ann had a new lease on life.

Three years later, I was walking through the hospital parking lot, when a pretty young woman, driving a red convertible, honked the horn and yelled my name. She parked her car and caught up to me.

"Hi Sue, you don't know who I am, do you?"

"No, I'm sorry. I don't recognize you."

"I'm Mary Ann Cunningham. You took care of me before my kidney transplant, remember?" I looked at her, hugged her and cried. She was so pretty. She had beautiful, shiny, blonde hair and looked so healthy. She was engaged to be married and feeling great. We talked awhile and then she headed off for her checkup.

I never saw Mary Ann again, but two years later a friend who worked in the dialysis unit, told me that Mary Ann had died. Her original kidney stopped working and she received a second one, but her body rejected the new one. I was very sad but also very glad that her life had been extended. She had the opportunity to live three or four more years without being sick all the time.

DR. JAMES, COME QUICK

"Sue, don't let me die!" It was 5:00a.m. on a cold, snowy, Sunday morning and Lisa and I had just started to take vital signs on our thirty-two bed, women's medical ward.

I worked permanent night duty with Jen, a licensed practical nurse, and Lisa, a nurse aide. Due to seniority, Jen had every Friday and Saturday night off.

We had four private rooms, a four-bed ward, an eight-bed ward and a sixteen-bed ward. All of the beds were filled because it was the only medical unit in a large university hospital.

During shift report, the evening nurse said, "Sue, I don't know what you are going to do with Marian tonight. I've given her every medicine she has for asthma and she's just getting wild in there. She keeps saying she needs to have intravenous Aminophylline. I'm sorry, Sue, good luck."

Lisa and I made rounds, and Mrs. Mertaugh, in Bed 4 of the sixteen-bed unit, was awake and crying. At the age of eighty-nine, she was being prepared to have her gall bladder out on Monday. She had dementia and was crying for her mommy. Marian was in Bed 8 and Mary Ann was in Room 4, waiting for a kidney transplant.

"How are you doing tonight, Marian?" I asked.

"Sue, you have to do something, I can't breathe. I need more medicine." I explained to her that she couldn't have any more medicine for at least three hours.

She kept wheezing and was really losing it, so at midnight I paged Dr. James, the intern on-call for our ward.

When he called back I told him that Marian had been given all of the "as needed" medications on the 3:00p.m. to 11:00 p.m. shift and was still in severe distress. Dr. James informed me that he was going skiing in the morning, he was not coming up to see Marian, and that I was not to call him again.

For the next three hours, Lisa and I took turns sitting with Marian, encouraging her to take slow breaths and try to relax. Nothing worked. She kept getting more and more anxious. At 4:00a.m., I paged Dr. James again. This time I had Lisa listen in on the conversation. I pleaded with him to come up to the ward and give Marian some Aminophylline. He yelled, "I told you not to call me again. If you want her to have Aminophylline, give it to her yourself."

"You know a nurse can't give intravenous medications," I said. With that he slammed down the phone.

Within minutes, the night supervisor arrived. I told her about Marian and Dr. James response when I called him both times. She told me to call the resident on-call and go over his head if Marian got worse. I had also charted on Marian's chart what Dr. James told me each time I called him. Lisa co-signed my second note as a witness.

At 5:00a.m. Lisa put thermometers in the mouths of the first eight patients. I was coming behind her, taking blood pressures when all of a sudden, Marian screamed, "Sue help me!" I ran to the phone and overhead paged the resident Dr. Lyons. I told him to come on the run. I also called Dr. James and said, "Hear that? That's Marian and she's hysterical."

I hung up the phone and ran to Marian. She took one look at me and said, "Sue don't let me die, don't let me die!" She was hysterical, so I grabbed her and pulled her up into a sitting position.

"Look at me, Marian!" I yelled. She was unable to focus on me because she was too out of control. Then I started to shake her to get her attention. While I was shaking her, I felt the presence of someone behind me. Her eyes went to the left of me and, after taking one breath, she slumped into my arms. Dr. James was standing behind me. Within seconds, Miss Takioshi, the night supervisor, and Dr. Lyons was there. Dr. James yelled for Lisa to overhead the anesthesiologist while we started CPR. The anesthesiologist arrived and intubated her, by putting a tube down her throat and into her lungs, so we could give her oxygen. Then she was rushed to the Medical Intensive Unit.

In shock, Lisa and I finished our early morning duties. I gave the day charge nurse my report and left the hospital. I didn't cry until I got home and then I cried myself to sleep.

One of my roommates, Melinda, worked the day shift on that same ward.

When she got home, she told me Marian was taken off the respirator at 11:00a.m. and pronounced dead. Melinda also said that Dr. James told everyone that "The damned nurse never called me until Marian was dying." I called in sick Sunday night, and on Monday I called the head nurse and asked to meet with her. I went in that afternoon. When I got there the head nurse and Dr. Weaver, an asthma specialist and the intern supervisor, met with me. We reviewed Marian's chart and guess what? My nurse's notes were missing. I told them that Lisa had listened to my second call to Dr. James. I also told the head nurse that I would never again work a Friday or Saturday night with just a nurse aide. I would leave the hospital and refuse to work if Jen's position wasn't covered. Dr. Weaver said he wanted to look into Marian's death more closely and we would meet again in one week. At our second meeting, Dr. Weaver said that he had put a portion of Marian's lung in water and it did not float. Because it didn't float, Dr. Weaver said that Marian died of hysteria not asthma. He also said that Marian had told her psychologist saturday morning that she thought she would die the next time she had an asthma attack. The psychologist didn't bother to write that information in her chart because Marian had been on our unit so many times and he didn't feel it was important.

Certainly my peers and I thought that Dr. James should have been reprimanded or perhaps even expelled from the intern program, but that never happened. I had nightmares of Marian yelling "Sue don't let me die!" for many months.

I will never forget Marian. She was just twenty-three years old when she died, and so was I. That was another incident that impacted my career and I learned a valuable lesson. I avoided working with asthmatics for many years.

Shortly after Marian's death I transferred to an adolescent psychiatric unit to learn more about how the mind can control the body without conscious thought.

WHO'S GUARDING THE KNIVES?

I woke up in a cold sweat. How could we have left all the knives out where Eloise could find them? After jumping out of bed, I realized that I was having that same old nightmare. I was at home and Eloise was in the hospital.

Eloise was sixteen-years old when I met her. She was an in-patient on an adolescent psychiatric unit of a big city hospital. With her beautiful, long, brown hair and athletic build she looked like any other teenager. That's where the resemblance ended.

The only child of two older professionals who found her to be a disruption to their lifestyle, she'd spent almost all of her life away from home. At age three, she was sent to a boarding school in South America. During summer vacations, she returned to the states and was sent to camp until it was time to return to boarding school. Over the Christmas holidays, she was sent on organized ski trips.

Is it any wonder that Eloise felt worthless, unlovable, and a complete failure? Every chance she got, she attempted to kill herself by cutting her wrists or neck. That's why she had spent almost two years on suicide precautions, meaning that she was within an arm's length of a staff member at all times, unless she was sleeping. At bedtime, every orifice was checked for any object with which she could hurt herself. She wore a patient gown that snapped shut and was escorted into a seclusion room where she slept on a bare mattress with a bulky blanket. The door was locked and she was observed through a 12" by 12" window every fifteen minutes while she was awake and every thirty minutes while she slept. I can't tell you how many times we found her in a pool of blood at the first fifteen minute check. She was a magician at hiding implements on her body or hair that she could use to cut herself.

I absolutely adored Eloise. She was bright, athletic, artistic and extremely intuitive. Many afternoons, when I was assigned to her, we went out to the basketball court. The two of us would play against three or four men from the forensic unit and beat them badly. Of course, those men were on large doses of medication which made it difficult for them to move quickly up and down the basketball court.

One time, Eloise and I both went up for a rebound and her head accidentally hit me in the jaw. I have the false tooth to prove it.

Eloise could draw anything. Since I have difficulty drawing stick figures, I was in awe of her ability. She often combined her art with her uncanny intuition.

Our unit had frequent parties and the patients always seemed to find out about them. Eloise would sit down and draw pictures of what she thought staff members were doing and who they were with at the party. She was so good that you could identify each staff member in her pictures. I remember one time she drew Holly, our head nurse, with Barry, a psychiatric technician. Guess what? Holly and Barry were dating and none of us knew it, but Eloise figured it out. Barry and Holly eventually married.

For two years, I had the same recurrent dream about Eloise and the knives.

Every time she succeeded in cutting herself, I felt sad for her. One time she told me that she would never try to hurt herself on a certain nurse's shift. I thought, what a lucky person and asked her why. She said, "I know she cares about us and I hate to see her upset." I asked her who the lucky nurse was and she said, "Don't you know? It's you." I can truthfully say that after that time, Eloise never tried to cut herself when I was on duty.

After working with Eloise for two years, we realized that when she started smiling, she was really depressed and needed to be watched more closely. In this day and age, Eloise would probably be taking an anti-depressant, but at that time there were no medications available to her.

Eloise turned eighteen and had to leave our facility. She was transferred to one of our state hospitals. We told her new staff that when she starts to smile, watch her closely. After one month, she was given a weekend pass with her parents. (I remember talking to Eloise's parents on the phone but never saw them visit her.)

The first night in her parents' home, she climbed out the window, took their car, and drove to a college football stadium. She climbed to the top and jumped off. She broke her pelvis, one leg and both arms. When our hospital staff heard about her, we were heart sick and overwhelmed with anger at the state hospital. However, a funny thing happened with Eloise. During her recovery, she stopped cutting on herself, but that only lasted until she recovered from her fractures.

Shortly after she jumped off the stadium, I left the state to get married and was gone for a year. When I returned to the adolescent unit, the staff was new and knew nothing about Eloise.

Six years later, I was working at a local Mental Health Center. We had a weekly meeting where we discussed clients who were apt to call the on-call team. A client named Linda was mentioned, and a male staff said, "She sounds just like Eloise." I almost fell off my chair. I yelled, "Are you talking about Eloise Miller?"

"Yes," he said. After the meeting, we had a long talk about Eloise, and guess what?

He also had nightmares about her. He had been working at the state hospital when Eloise jumped off the stadium and six years later she was still there. Over the next three years, we heard rumors about her being re-parented by two nurses who were roommates. The story went that when they were both at work, Eloise would be at the hospital, but when one or both of them were at home, Eloise would be in their home, one night while one nurse was working night duty, the other nurse woke up with Eloise standing over her with a knife. That was the end of the re-parenting.

In 1984, eight years later, I was supervising two psychiatric units in a private hospital and met back up with Madge. Madge and I had worked with Eloise on the adolescent unit. One day, while reminiscing about some of the adolescents with whom we had worked, I asked her if she ever heard anything about Eloise. She told me that both of Eloise's parents were dead and that Eloise had become a paramedic. Madge said that Eloise even brought patients to our units for admission. She had moved to another state two years prior to our conversation.

It was gratifying to hear that Eloise had been able to overcome all her sadness and self hate and become a productive member of society by helping others. I always thought that with her intelligence and intuition, Eloise could be successful in any field she chose after putting her past behind her. Eloise, you deserve the best. Wherever you are, I pray you are happy.

A WEEK ON EAST TWO

"Karen, quick, come with me." I couldn't believe my eyes when I walked out of the nurses' station and saw Karen standing in the middle of the hall wearing only a white half-slip, tucked up under her arms.

I put my arm around her shoulder and started to lead her to the girls' dormitory. She stopped and said, "I'm pure, aren't I? I'm wearing white. See, I'm clean." It was Friday evening, and ten of the sixteen patients on the adolescent psychiatric unit had visitors. They were everywhere, in the dayroom, standing in the hall, and walking through the front door. I had to get more clothes on Karen.

Karen was sixteen-years old, diagnosed with schizophrenia. In her mind, she was just fine dressed in her white half-slip. After all, white is the color of purity. She had been sexually abused at age four by her uncle. I can only imagine how her family reacted to the assault since she was reacting like this twelve years later. I've always believed that a small child's reaction to any situation is dependent upon how the adults around them react.

After I convinced Karen to put on more clothes, visiting hours went more smoothly. However, the calm mood didn't last long. At 9:00 p.m., after visiting hours were over, Jenny came running down the hall to get me. She said her roommate had taken an overdose of pills that she had stolen from a nearby pharmacy while on pass. I asked Merg, my fifty-five year old psychiatric technician, to get Terri and bring her to the treatment room. I would need to give her some Ipecac syrup, and then call the resident on-call. Again, Jenny came to get me. Terri had kicked Merg in the stomach. Well, I'd been raised to respect your elders, and I saw red when I heard what happened.

My reputation on the unit was that of the "smiley nurse" who never got mad.

When some of my peers swore at the patients, I was appalled and felt it was very unprofessional. That was about to change.

I walked into Terri's room and told her to get out of bed and come with me.

She just laughed at me and that made me furious. I found myself saying, "Damn it, Terri, get up and get to the treatment room." She looked up at me and said to Jenny, "Sue really can get mad." She got up and headed for the treatment room.

Since she had just ingested the over-the-counter sleeping pills, they came right back up with the Ipecac syrup.

Terri came from a small home town and, at fifteen, she was the leader of the town's gang. Initially, I was intimidated by her size and swagger. However, when she confided in me that she wanted to learn how to walk, talk, and act like a lady, I wanted to help her.

Three days later, we got a new patient, Cherie. When I interviewed her and asked her what she would like to change about herself, she said, "My looks, I'm ugly."

Cherie was a homely-looking adolescent, but her sense of humor was very endearing. She had few social skills and didn't know how to ask for what she needed without acting out. Early one evening, she walked up to the nurses' office and broke the window with her fist. The glass shattered and hit our ward clerk, Bee, in the face. While someone took Bee to the emergency room, I dealt with Cherie. She had some small cuts on her knuckles so I took her to the treatment room.

Cherie also had a psychotic diagnosis. However, I felt she needed to be responsible for her behavior. I asked her how she would feel if Bee got glass in her eyes and went blind. She started to cry and said, "I didn't want to hurt anyone, I just wanted some attention."

I told her I would spend time with her anytime she asked, but not if she didn't ask appropriately. We practiced how she could ask for attention. After that talk, when we got together we did a lot of exercising. The day she was discharged, I hugged her and wished her good luck. With a gleam in her eye, she said, "Keep up the exercising, Sue."

We had just finished dinner and I was back on the ward with half of the kids and Max was still in the cafeteria with the rest of them. When I walked into the dayroom, Cindy was threatening another patient. I told her to stop and take a timeout. She grabbed a pool cue and started swinging it at me. Somehow, I got behind her and put her in a bear hug so that she couldn't raise her arms. I yelled at one of the kids to go get Max. Cindy was a big girl and she was flinging me around like a rag doll. When Max arrived, he took the pool cue out of her hands and we walked her to a seclusion room to cool off.

Cindy had been sexually abused by her father for a number of years. Her mother knew about it, but did nothing. As a result, she was filled with rage and mistrusted all adults, especially women. She kept people from getting close to to her by threatening to hurt them. She had some of our nurses afraid of her, so when they set a limit with her and she broke that limit, they looked the other way. I didn't look the other way and followed through with consequences when she tested me.

Dr C. asked me to co-lead his adolescent group that Cindy was a part of.

When we all sat down, Cindy glared at me, and according to Dr. C., I glared right back at her. Dr. C. started the group by saying, "Well Cindy, you said if Sue came to group you would hurt her. What's that all about?"

My mouth fell open and I looked at Dr. C. as if to say, "Why didn't you warn me?"

Cindy looked down for about thirty seconds and then said, "Actually, Sue is a cool head. When she says if I break a rule I will have a consequence, she means it."

When other nurses tell me that and I break the rule, they look the other way."

"So what does that mean to you, Cindy?"

"It means that Sue really cares. She wants me to do good because she cares about me."

Boy, was I ever relieved. That wasn't what I expected Cindy to say. Her statement only reinforced my feeling that adolescents look for and want limits. So when I walked onto the ward on Saturday morning and the first kid up said, "Don't anyone breathe wrong, Sue's working today." I responded by saying, "I know, that's just your way of saying you like it when I'm here."

MARIA'S STORY

Today we were getting a new resident on the adolescent psychiatric unit and I was to be her primary nurse. I was excited about meeting a new child and the challenges that would lie ahead. The first few weeks were always the hardest.

With a smile on my face and my hand outstretched, I entered the intake room. "Hi Maria, Welcome to CPH," I said. "I'm Sue, and I'll be your primary nurse while you're here." Believe me, I wasn't prepared for what happened next!

All of a sudden I found myself on my back on the floor with Maria straddling me.

She was pulling my hair with one hand and hitting me in the face with the other one.

Her father released her hand from my hair and he and Dorothy, the social worker, pulled her off of me. He held her in a bear hug for the remainder of the interview.

Maria was fourteen-years old when she came to CPH in 1964. According to her family, she had had measles with encephalitis while in second grade. After that she was very disruptive in the classroom, destroying property and assaulting her classmates. She was kicked out of the school district in the third grade. Maria had two older brothers who played sports and were successful in school. Both of her parents worked, so what to do with Maria during the day became a big issue. I can't recall if Maria had a home tutor from school, but I know for sure that she'd had no formal education for at least four years prior to coming to CPH.

The family chose to solve the problem by locking Maria in her room day and night. She was given a small child's potty-chair, and food was passed through a small opening in the door on a tray. To this day, I can't believe that no one missed Maria or wondered about her whereabouts. As a result of such treatment, Maria was like a scared animal when I first met her.

On admission, Maria was moved into a seclusion room where she would stay for the next nine months. The room was about twelve feet long and nine feet wide, with no furniture except for a bare mattress on the floor. The door was locked from the outside with a one-foot-square window at the top for observation purposes.

Maria continued to be very aggressive, like a frightened, cornered animal.

Daily activities such as bathing and putting on clean clothes took at least three female staff members. Believe me, there were many times when I got wetter then Maria. In addition to pulling hair, Maria had a knack for breaking eyeglasses.

Every time we approached her, those wearing glasses had to take them off. Our head nurse couldn't see at all without her glasses, so she bought at least three pairs of glasses during Maria's stay on East Two. Since Maria was so aggressive and we couldn't spend any time with her alone, the psychiatrist decided to try Thorazine, a major tranquilizer and antipsychotic medication. Maria was not psychotic but Thorazine was given to her because she was filled with rage. She was about five-feet-four inches tall and weighed about one hundred-ten pounds but she was extremely strong. I can remember that at one time Maria was on 2400mg of Thorazine, and it never slowed her down. It did, however, cause her to gain fifty pounds.

As Maria became more comfortable with each of us, we started taking her out of her room and introducing her to the milieu. Her doctor decided that she should start attending a group that was held behind a one-way mirror. Two of us would take Maria to the group room and restrain her to a chair using chest, arm and ankle restraints. The restraints didn't seem to phase Maria. She was able to move the chair so that she could get close enough to another resident to kick or spit on them. She also spit on everyone who passed her when she was sitting in a chair outside her room. One day, I was really tired of being spit on, so I went to the water fountain and got about two tablespoons of water in a paper cup. As I passed by Maria, she spit on me, and I threw the cold water in her face. It ran down her face and onto her shirt. I told her that from then on every time she spit on me I would throw cold water on her. She never spat on me again but continued to spit on everyone else. We decided to make a hood made out of a pillow case with only holes in it for eyes. If she tried to spit on people, she would be the one to get wet and uncomfortable.

One day while watching the group through the one way mirror, the psychiatrist said, "Sue, come in here and get Maria. She keeps kicking people and is too disruptive." I went to the door and pulled Maria out into the hall, chair and all, but now I had a dilemma. There was no way I could take Maria back to the ward by myself. Leaving Maria alone, hooded and restrained, I ran about twenty feet to the nearest adult ward to call for assistance. When I returned I came across Dr. J. a well known forensic psychiatrist, talking to Maria. As I approached he yelled, "Unmask this child, this is not the dark ages."

"I'm not sure that's a good idea, Dr. J., Maria has a spitting problem."

He then asked my name and said he was going to have me fired. Again he ordered me to remove Maria's hood.

As I removed the hood, Maria sucked in her saliva and spat a huge "hocker" right into Dr. J's face. He screamed something in Scottish and ran down the hall with his hands over his face. A fellow staff member arrived and we took Maria back to East Two. After getting her settled, I talked to our ward chief, Dr. B. I asked him if another psychiatrist other than himself could fire me. He asked why, and I told him about Dr. J's response to Maria's hood and his threat towards me.

Dr. B. mumbled something about how Dr. J. should deal with the murderers on his own unit and went looking for him. I don't know what happened after that, because nothing further was said to me and Maria continued to wear her hood.

Maria's aggression continued to lessen and soon one person was able to take her from place to place, un-hooded and unrestrained. However, you had to give her your total attention. I remember taking her into the dayroom for a community meeting. We were seated side by side when another resident asked me a question. I turned to look at him and the next thing I knew, I was being pulled our of my chair by my hair. It hurt so much that I cried. I had a bald spot there for quite a while.

After nine months, it was decided that Maria needed therapy for a much longer time. A referral was made for Maria to go to the state hospital. Her parents were furious.

"You're not sending our child to the state hospital. That's for crazy people," they said. They signed Maria out of the hospital against medical advice and took her back home. We were all very worried about Maria because we knew what awaited her back home. She was such a bright child and basically self-taught.

About three years later, the state hospital was opening a new adolescent unit.

They'd always had a children's unit but not one for adolescents. Due to my involvement in groups, recreation therapy and interest, I was the nurse chosen to go with Dr. B. and the social worker, as consultants to their new unit. We were touring the facility, and standing in the middle of this huge gym when a door flew open and someone yelled, "Sue, Sue, it's you." Next thing I knew, I was in a bear hug and the breath was being squeezed out of me.

I gasped, "Who is it?" and our tour guide told me it was Maria. I was so glad to see her. She had gone home and destroyed her parents' home in a very short time. That convinced her parents that she needed long-term treatment and they took her to the state hospital. According to the staff, Maria was no longer assaulting people. She still got mad and was filled with rage but was able to remove herself from the situation and go to her room when that happened.

Maria, I've thought of you so often over the years. Where are you now?

FLYING HIGH

It was Saturday night and there wasn't much happening on the adolescent psych unit, so the psych technician decided to drive the residents around to look at the Christmas lights. After awhile, we decided to park the hospital van beside the airport's East/West runway, to watch planes land. We'd been sitting there for about fifteen minutes when we saw the plane lights coming towards us.

All of a sudden Brad, a twelve-year old boy, yelled "Everybody get down, we're going to be killed."

He was inconsolable from that moment on. I told my co-worker that we had to get back to the hospital fast. When we got back to the hospital, Brad was still crying and mumbling incoherently. If I had known then what I know now about PTSD (Post Traumatic Stress Disorder) we would never have been anywhere near the airport.

I worked on a sixteen-bed psychiatric unit in a university hospital. Brad had come to us that same year with a diagnosis of psychosis.

Brad's natural father, a navy jet pilot, had crashed and died on a training mission when Brad was just five-years old. On admission, Brad was out of touch with reality. He saw bugs crawling everywhere. On a bad day, he would undress and run down the hall in the nude with arms extended thinking he was a jet plane.

He thought if he ran into you he would kill you.

In view of his psychotic behavior, he was sometimes removed from the rest of the group. He became more confused by a lot of activity. When male staff sat with him, his descriptions of crawling bugs on the window screen were so vivid that with within fifteen minutes they also saw the bugs.

Over the course of the year, Brad regressed to the point of bowel and bladder incontinence and behaved like a toddler. I'm not sure to this day what or how we did it but we gradually rebuilt his psyche.

On January 9th that next year, my husband was killed in Vietnam. The plane he was in was shot down. I went back to Pennsylvania immediately to be with our respective families. I was there for over three weeks because it took so long to get his body back home. I received flowers and cards from the staff and residents but one letter I still hold close to my heart. It was from Brad.

His letter simply said, "Dear Sue, they tell me that your husband's plane was shot down in Vietnam. No one knows if you will be coming back here. I only hope if you do, I can help you as much as you helped me. I was really little when my dad died but I remember what my mom went through."

I did return and on my first day back, Brad came up to me, and touching my arm as if to see what it was made of, said, "It's really you, Sue. I'm so glad you came back."

I couldn't understand why Brad touched me and later asked Dr. B. about it.

He said that even though Brad had written a coherent letter, he wasn't sure I was real until he touched me. Dr. B. further explained that since I had left so abruptly, perhaps in Brad's mind I had died and not my husband.

I was so glad to be back. I had just spent three weeks wandering around aimlessly in limbo. I needed the structure of work to get myself grounded again.

The very next day I was to work from 10:00a.m. until 6:30 p.m. When I arrived at the ward door, it was locked. Holly, my head nurse, and Dr. B. opened the door and joined me in the hall.

"You don't have to come to work today, Sue. We want you to take a couple of days off." Dr. B said.

"Oh, yes I do. What's wrong? Why can't I go onto the ward?" They both sputtered a bit, and I kept insisting I was there to work.

They finally leveled with me. The night before, a sixteen-year old boy had hanged and killed himself in his room. He and a young girl had run away, and when they returned the girl told the staff that they had had s sexual encounter while on the run. There was no suicide note so we surmised that he was afraid of the possible consequences.

I did go to work that day. My peers thought that the suicide would further upset me but it didn't. In hindsight, I realize that I was in shock and the two deaths had nothing in common for me. We had several group meetings that day with the other residents to talk about the suicide. At one point, Dr. B. asked everyone, "What do you think we should do now?"

Brad looked over at me and in a very caring way suggested that it was time to send flowers again.

Soon it was my turn to work nights. The permanent night psych tech, Howard, was the person who found the boy who had hung himself. Looking back, we were quite a pair to be working together. He had constant nightmares and I cried all the time. However, I think we helped each other. Soon his nightmares subsided to a point that he wasn't afraid to go to sleep. My self-esteem had hit rock bottom, and Howard and I argued about my worth as a human being. I truly believe that if you are told something repeatedly that you start to believe it. I want to thank Howard for telling me that I was a neat person with a lot to offer others.

About nine moths later, Brad was discharged. He went back home to live with his mother, step-dad and siblings. Over the years, I've met people who know Brad and understand that he has never had another psychotic episode. Working with Brad was one of the most rewarding experiences of my nursing career.

GLUE DOESN'T ALWAYS HOLD THINGS TOGETHER

"Eddie, put that bat down!" I was working with adolescents from a psychiatric unit and we were outside playing softball. Eddie had been with us for about a month. He was admitted because of his outbursts. They seemed to come out of no where and when we least expected them. He had been sniffing glue to get high for about two years.

We had to be very watchful when Eddie got hurt because glue apparently thins the blood. He would bleed easily and stopping it was difficult.

It was Eddie's turn to bat. Strike one, strike two. He was so uncoordinated that his bat didn't come close to hitting the ball. Max, the pitcher, threw the ball at bat but he struck out. "Strike three! Eddie you're out." All of a sudden, Eddie began chasing Max, swinging the bat in the air trying to hit him in the head. I had visions of Max laying on the ground unconscious and bleeding. So, I started running after Eddie. I was yelling at him to put down the bat. He kept running and I kept yelling.

Eventually, I got his attention and had almost caught up with him when he turned around and yelled, "Get back, Sue I don't want to hurt you." At this point, he was swinging the bat waist high. I kept running after him and soon he turned and threw the bat at my legs. I jumped over it and put my hand on his shoulder "Come on, Eddie, we're going back to the ward. You're scaring me and everyone else." He turned and starting walking back to the building with me. He allowed me to keep my hand on his shoulder the whole way to the ward. Our ward was on the second floor so we had to take the stairs. While we were going up the steps, Max was at the reception desk calling the adult units for help. As Eddie and I entered the ward, I told him that I wanted him to spend some time in the seclusion room until he got himself under better control. We were about ten feet from the seclusion room when the ward door flew open and eight males came running in.

Eddie freaked out and ran to the end of the hall where he was cornered. They took him down to the floor, and held him until he was calm enough to walk to the seclusion room. They locked the door and left. I felt so bad that Eddie had been restrained. If only the male staff had waited until I got Eddie into the seclusion room before storming the ward. I know that they were concerned about my safety, and I was very appreciative, but the restraint could have been avoided. I walked to the seclusion room and asked him if was okay. We talked through the door for a few minutes and then told him I would be back to check on him in fifteen minutes.

Twenty years later, I was supervising two adult psychiatric units and attempting to collect data to confirm the need for more male staff on the unit with psychotic patients. Guess what? The research data indicated that it is actually best to have more females because psychotic males don't get as aggressive with females.

They don't have to prove their machismo with women.

Eddie continued to have explosive outbursts. We also realized that his nervous system had become short circuited from sniffing glue, and that was the reason for his poor coordination. He stayed with us for another month or so and then was transferred to the state psychiatric hospital. I've wondered many times what became of Eddie.

Two years later, I was working in the Emergency Room of a small community hospital in Michigan. We repeatedly saw a teenage boy with nose bleeds that would not stop on their own. We packed his nose several times.

A month after seeing him for the fourth time, a female cousin was admitted to the hospital by way of the emergency room. Her diagnosis was continual vaginal bleeding. I started thinking about Eddie and asked their physician if they could be sniffing glue. Sure enough, both of them had been sniffing glue for a period of time. I can't remember what happened to those two teenagers, but I do know there were no drug, alcohol or psychiatric services in that small town.

MR. McDUGGIN DID WHAT?

In 1966 I worked in a small community hospital in the Upper Peninsula of Michigan. When Jane, the evening nurse, gave me her report, she told me that she was most concerned about Mr. McDuggin. He was an elderly gentleman who had a hernia repair four days earlier. This morning, Dr. Hayes had taken out his stitches and now he was coughing a lot. Jane told me that she had given Mr. McDuggin some Elixir of Terpin Hydrate, twice to quell his cough. I decided to do the same on my shift. So at midnight and 4:00 a.m. when I took his vital signs, I gave him more cough syrup.

The night was slow. Pat, the nurse aide, and I were making Christmas tree ornaments. I couldn't afford store-bought ornaments, so we were rolling used plastic medicine cups in glitter and putting paper clips through their bottoms in order to hang them. About 4:45a.m. Mr. McDuggin's light went on.

"I'll get that," Pat said. "You just keep working on your ornaments."

She returned in fifteen seconds, her face so pale she looked like she might faint. "Get in there right away, Sue. He's laying there with blood all over his stomach!"

Mr. McDuggen had coughed so much he had eviscerated.

"EVISCERATION!" That was my worst fear for surgical patients. Stay calm, I told myself; get some sterile dressings, make them moist with sterile normal saline, reassure Mr. McDuggin, and call Dr. Hayes.

But there was no normal saline on the floor. I called, Mrs. Long, the night supervisor. She was in the delivery room delivering a baby since the Dr. had not yet made it to the hospital "Send Pat down here," she said, "and she can get the key out of my pocket and get the saline."

While I waited for the saline, I called Dr. Hayes. "Dr. Hayes, I'm Sue Fritz and I'm calling you about Mr. McDuggin." There was no answer. Dr. Hayes had gone back to sleep.

"Dr. Hayes," I shouted.

"What?"

"This is the hospital calling about Mr. McDuggin. The contents of his abdomen are laying on the outside," I said.

"What?"

"In short sir, he has eviscerated."

"<u>EVISERATION</u>" He yelled. He must have slammed down the phone because the phone went dead.

Now what was I going to do? I called Mrs. Long back. She said, "Don't worry, Sue. Dr Hayes bas a tendency to panic. He'll call you back and tell you to pre-op Mr. McDuggin and call anesthesia and the operating room." As we were hanging up the other line was ringing. "This is Dr. Hayes. Give Mr. McDuggin 25mg of Phenergan and 50mg of Demerol. Call the OR staff and the Anesthesiologist. Tell Mr. McDuggin I'll be right in."

"Okay, but I don't think your going to need an anesthesiologist. I think you can close him up under a local anesthesia."

"Okay, cancel the anesthesiologist." With that, he slammed the phone down.

Pat returned with the saline. The wet dressings were applied, Mr. McDuggin was cleaned up, and given the pre-op medications. Since he was in a four bed unit it was imperative not to disturb the other three patients. Mr. Johnson, the man directly across the room from the foot of Mr. McDuggin's bed, had a heart attack three days after his surgery. A sign was posted above his bed <u>DO NOT STARTLE</u>.

This community hospital had only one hundred and twenty beds and no intensive care unit, which was where Mr. Johnson should have been.

About 5:30 a.m, Pat started to make rounds giving everyone fresh water and ice. As I sat there rolling a cup in red glitter, a tall, thin, gray haired man wearing operating green scrubs walked up. I said, "Dr. Hayes, I presume! I'm Miss Fritz and I'm new here."

"From New Orleans?"

"No sir, I said I'm Miss Fritz and I'm new here."

"From New Orleans?"

No one told me he was deaf, I thought. "No sir" I shouted, "I said...."

"I know what you said," He shouted back. "I asked you three times, are you from New Orleans?"

"No, sir, I'm from Pennsylvania."

"Then, where did you get that southern accent. My wife is from Pennsylvania and she doesn't talk like that."

"I don't have a southern accent. Don't you think you should see Mr. McDuggin now?"

"Of course," he answered and headed for the patient's room. I followed right behind him.

As he turned on the light above Mr. McDuggin's bed, I reached down to pull the curtain at the foot of his bed. Dr. Hayes grabbed the curtain separating Mr. McDuggin from the bed beside his. Looking back over his shoulder and talking to Mr. McDuggin, he jerked the curtain closed just as I was turning around.

POW! Dr. Hayes socked me in the chin with such force that I flew backward onto the foot of Mr. Johnson's bed.

"Oh my God, nurse! Are you okay?"

"I'm fine, just take care of Mr. McDuggin."

Dr. Hayes took Mr. McDuggin's bed down the hall toward the surgery suite.

I gave my report to the day charge nurse and left the hospital Mr. McDuggin recovered without anymore problems. Not all of my interactions with Dr. Hayes were that chaotic. In fact, we became friends and often laughed about our first meeting.

A NURSE'S DILEMMA

It was 10:45p.m. when I walked into the dimly lit nurses' station on 2 West.

Ellen, the evening nurse, put a finger to her lips as if to say "BE QUIET" and pulled me into the medicine room. "Who's that man asleep at the desk in the nurses' station?" I asked.

"That's Dr. Moxie and he's been waiting for you since 10:00 o'clock. I overheard Mrs. Sanders in 204 Bed A tell him you were mean to her last night."

She said you wouldn't give her any medication to sleep and she cried all night.

"Sue be really careful, Dr. Moxie can be really mean. He could have you fired."

I paused for a while to collect my thoughts. Well, I told Mrs. Sanders that I wanted to talk to him so I guess this is my chance. I decided that I had to be really confident. After all, he was the one in the wrong. I felt I had only done what any responsible nurse would have done under the circumstance. It was my nurse's license in jeopardy not his.

I grabbed the medication book, Mrs. Sander's chart, and turned on the overhead light as I hurried into the nurses' station. "Dr. Moxie, I'm Sue, the night nurse, I'm glad I got a chance to talk to you."

"What! Huh!" he gasped as he struggled to wake up and focus.

"I wanted to talk to you about Mrs. Sanders. Do you have any idea what she has been using for sleep for the last six weeks?"

"Well, let's see. I think I ordered Chloral Hydrate for her."

"Right, that's what you ordered but that's not what she's getting. When she came in you wanted to rule out a fractured hip and arthritis. The original order was Demerol 50mg (IM) for pain. That order was never discontinued."

"Dr. Moxie, my mother has been in a wheelchair for twenty-five years with arthritis and Aspirin helps her pain better then any narcotic. Mrs. Sanders has been getting 50 mg of Demerol every night at bedtime. I'm not a physician or a pharmacist and I don't know how much time and Demerol it takes to addict someone, but Mrs. Sanders is seventy-eight years old and only weighs eighty-five pounds. Who will give her a Demerol shot every night when she goes home in a couple of weeks? As a nurse, I won't be a part of addicting her."

"That can't be. We ruled out a fractured hip so she doesn't need Demerol. Surely, she's not still getting it."

"Look for yourself. It's right here in her chart and the medication book."

"Good lord, thank you for bringing this to my attention. I support your decision. I'll go talk to Mrs. Sanders right now and explain why I don't want her to have any more Demerol."

Dr. Moxie went directly to Room 204. He returned to the nurses' station in fifteen minutes and sheepishly said, "I want you to give her 25mg of Sparine (IM) for three nights and then discontinue all shots at bedtime. And of course, I'm discontinuing the Demerol. You're new here aren't you? I don't remember meeting you before."

"I started about six weeks ago and work night duty so I don't get a chance to meet many physicians."

"Welcome aboard Sue, we need more nurses like you. Good night now."

When I returned to work the next night, 2 West was buzzing. Everyone wanted to know how I got the nerve to stand up to the dreaded Dr. Moxie. During the night, Mrs. Long, the night supervisor, stopped by to tell me she'd heard about the Mrs. Sanders incident and that Dr. Moxie had stopped by her office to tell her how pleased he was with my care of Mrs. Sanders.

The only person who wasn't happy was Mrs. Sanders. She was irritable and couldn't sleep for a couple of nights. Could it be that she was having signs of withdrawal?

WHAT COULD I HAVE BEEN DOING?

It was 10:55p.m. when I arrived for my night shift. Sally, the evening nurse, told me to go into Room 240 because Johnny was waiting up to talk to me. I had no idea why he wanted to see me, but went right into his room.

"I know where I saw you before," Johnny said. "It was May of 1964, and you and another girl were riding in a green 1960 Chevrolet on the base at Fort Riley, Kansas."

Needless to say, I was dumbfounded. I indeed had been on the base at Fort Riley in 1964. I wanted to talk more, but knew I needed the evening report from Sally, so I told him we'd talk more in the morning.

He had frost bite on his hands, nose and feet. We did not allow him to have a mirror because of the way his face looked. Black and dry, his nose looked like it was going to fall off his face at any minute. I remember following his doctor down the hall and asking him what I should do when his nose falls off.

"His nose is not going to fall off," Dr. Ventura said.

"Are you sure? It looks like it to me, and I'm the one who will be here, not you."

Johnny had two fingers on one hand and one toe removed before gangrene set in.

The night supervisor's husband, Max, and Johnny had gone ice fishing. The chunk of ice they were on had broken away from the lake, and they were stranded.

Johnny kept saying, "I survived two tours in Vietnam and now, I'm going to die here." Max kept telling him to keep moving around, but Johnny kept lying down on the ice.

"My wife will call home soon. When she doesn't get an answer, she'll call the sheriff," Max said. That is exactly what happened. Max was evaluated in the emergency room and discharged. He had no frost bite, due to moving around.

The first night I met Johnny, he told me he knew me from somewhere. I asked him if he ever lived in Colorado or Pennsylvania? He said, "No." I joked and told him I had one of those familiar faces and forgot about our conversation.

The next morning Johnny and I talked more. To this day, I'm amazed that he remembered me. My roommate and I were only on the base for fifteen minutes to pick up a friend. What on earth could I have been doing to draw attention to myself?

Johnny's nose never fell off, at least while he was in the hospital. After his discharge, I never saw him again. But, who knows if he ever saw me again.

WAS SHE A DISILLUSIONED MISTRESS OR JUST AN ANGRY WOMAN?

Dr. Ventura was beloved by the entire community. In fact, out of fourteen physicians in this small town, he had fifty percent of the patients. He was overworked and spent entirely too much time at our hospital.

It was no surprise that he had a massive heart attack and became my patient.

He had such a wonderful sense of humor that we all loved joking with him. When he had somewhat recovered from his heart attack and was preparing to leave the hospital, Dr. Moxie, his cardiologist, told him that he needed to take at least two months off work. Dr. Moxie suggested that he leave town so he wouldn't be tempted to return too soon.

So, Dr. Ventura decided to go to Florida. That was a wonderful idea since our average temperature was—14 degrees that winter. Several of us nurses volunteered to accompany him to Florida. We said we didn't want him to overdo too quickly.

Dr. Ventura was discharged from the hospital, and a week later came by to say goodbye and thank us for his care. I told him it wouldn't take me long to pack and he just laughed. He said when he called for plane reservations for two, the airline asked if the reservation was for Dr. and Mrs. Ventura. He replied no.

Because we had all joked around about going with him, he said he'd just let them imagine who was going with him. In truth, it was his father-in-law.

Later that morning, I accompanied Dr. Moxie and his partner, Dr. Helen Maclaughlin, on rounds, to see their patients. Dr. Moxie laughingly told her that I was upset because I couldn't go along with Tom Ventura to Florida. I pretended to pout and he just laughed.

Dr. Maclaughlin was a tall, thin, grim looking, humorless lady. She was unmarried but the hospital grapevine claimed she had once had a ten-year affair with another married physician.

After Dr. Moxie left our nursing unit, Dr. Maclaughlin grabbed my arm and said, "Young woman, don't you think you're playing with fire?" With that said, she turned and walked away, not allowing me to explain that it was just a joke. I soon forgot the incident, but apparently Dr. Maclaughlin did not.

For the next several weeks, every time she walked onto my unit there was trouble. She would yell, "Miss Fritz, why didn't my patient in Room 235 get her bedtime snack? I'm tired of you nurses and your sloppy nursing care." I explained to her that I didn't come to work until 11:00 p.m. and that I would try to find out what happened and someone would get back to her. Our interactions were always explosive, and I never understood why. Almost all of her complaints were about something that happened on another shift but I was always her target.

Looking back, I wonder if Dr. Maclaughlin didn't realize that Dr. Moxie was joking. Was she a disillusioned mistress or just an angry woman?

THE ECLIPSE OF MY HEART

I'd been at work on the adolescent psychiatric unit for about forty-five minutes when the office phone rang. Claire, the Director of Nursing Service, asked me to come down to her office right away.

Jokingly I said, "Claire, I didn't do it, I didn't do it, I didn't do it but I'm on my way." I skipped down a flight of steps and went right towards her office.

As I entered Claire's office, I saw Claire looking nervously down at the floor.

A priest and an Air Force officer with lots of bars on his uniform were with her.

Knowing immediately why the two men were there, I turned around and ran out the door, down the hall, out the side door, across the parking lot and down the middle of 8th avenue. My heart told me it was true but my head said "Run. If they can't catch you it's not true." I ran as fast and as far as I could, dodging oncoming cars with three male co-workers in hot pursuit. They eventually caught up with me, and with their arms around me and soothing voices, they walked me back to Claire's office.

They sat me in an arm chair and the Air Force officer told me that my husband, Lonny, had been killed in Vietnam. Puff the Magic Dragon, the plane he was in, was shot down by ground fire and all seven crewmen were dead. I remember crying, "No, no," and clinging to the office wall. I felt so alone. Soon, Dr. Barber, our ward chief, had his arms around me and was saying, "It's over Sue, you don't have to worry anymore." The next forty-five minutes were a blur to me, and then I was back in my apartment with my ex-roommate and her current roommate.

I called my parents in Pennsylvania and they asked Rae if she could fly home with me. She agreed and while she made plane reservations for the next day, I attempted to pack my suitcase. Looking through my mail

I found two letters and an audio tape from Lonny "See," I said, "he can't be dead, he's talking to me." The tape was seven days old but to me it was proof that he was still alive. Within minutes, Rae's roommate said, "Let's get the hell out of here. There's nothing else we can do here." I was so hurt that she couldn't see that I didn't want to be alone, but was too numb to say anything.

Rae and I flew home the next morning. My father was crying when he picked us up at the airport. He took me directly to Lonny's parents' home then drove Rae to her home. I entered the house through the garage and noticed that it was eerily quiet. When I came into the living room, there was Gerald, Lonny's father, Mildred, Lonny's mother, and Debbie, his little sister sitting on the long couch. When Gerald jumped up and ran across the room to embrace me, Mildred fell over on her side in a sitting position. She was catatonic. She had not moved on her own or spoken in twelve hours. Grandma, Sophie, and sister, Bonnie, were huddled together on the love seat weeping quietly.

I spent the next nine days in true limbo, splitting my time between my parents' home and Lonny's home. Since I was a nurse, I spent time working with Mildred, to get her out of, that catatonic state.

Staying with my parents was almost unbearable. They were very emotional and every time they looked at me they started to cry. My best friend, Rosemary, arrived within two days and helped me keep what little sanity I had left. She would take me for long rides while I cried my eyes out. Seven days into the unbearable wait, Lonny's casket arrived escorted by a military guard. His casket had been sealed in Vietnam, not to be opened again.

There is no humor in planning a funeral but now, forty-two years later, I can laugh. We were sitting in the living room and the funeral director was giving us options and asking us questions. When he asked, what was Lonny's favorite flower?

I immediately said red carnations and Mildred said yellow roses. Can you imagine a casket blanket made with that mixture? The second question was what was his favorite hymn? I said "America the Beautiful" and Mildred said "Rock of Ages."

Obviously we were both naming our favorites. At this point, Rosemary looked over at the military guard, and he rolled his eyes while both of them held back giggles.

In the end, the coffin blanket was composed of white roses and red carnations.

Four days later, we buried Lonny. His minister and my uncle David, who had married us, performed the service. Before people arrived, I demanded that Lonny's casket be opened so I could be sure he was in there. Uncle David said, "Absolutely not." He had been a pastor during the Korean Conflict and said there may only be a leg or Lonny's dog tags and rocks in the casket. He then said, "Susan, God only gives burdens to people who can handle them."

"Well, this time He blew it. I can't and I won't accept Lonny's death," I said.

Naturally, I lost that battle, but not being able to see Lonny's body allowed me to hope that he had not been killed. I have learned not to judge people who are grieving. One day while waiting for Lonny's body to come back from Vietnam, twelve-year old Debbie looked at her grandmother and said, "Why couldn't you have died instead of Lonny?" Sophie was very hurt and I'm sure she would have changed places with Lonny if she could have.

After the funeral, we went back to the house. I remember exchanging jokes with one of my cousins. Many times over the years, I've wondered what Lonny's friends and family thought of my behavior.

I did some crazy things while I was in shock. I think God puts people in shock so that they can get through the death of a loved one and brings them out of shock when they can deal with the grief. On the plane, on the way back to Denver, I took off my wedding and engagement rings and said "When something is over it's over." My seat-mates asked if I had gotten a divorce. With no emotion, I told them that my husband had been killed in Vietnam three weeks ago.

After the shock wore off, I saw Lonny everywhere. I would call my roommate, Rosemary, and tell her that I was on my way home from work. Then I would see someone driving in the opposite direction that looked like Lonny. I would make a u-turn and chase that car until I could see he wasn't Lonny. Arriving an hour later, Rosemary would be upset with me because our dinner was cold or over cooked. I thought I was losing my mind. I'd tell Rosemary that one of the kids acted up and I had to help restrain him.

Three years later I remarried. When the POW's came home, I found myself glued to the television set looking for Lonny. I didn't see him but that's when the nightmares began. Every other night for about two weeks, I dreamed that Lonny rang our doorbell. When I opened the door he said, "I know you think I'm dead but I'm alive and I want you back." In my dreams, I would tell Lonny that my new husband had been terribly hurt by his first wife and I couldn't hurt him, too. I would wake myself up crying. My new husband, Dave, wanted to know why I was crying. I would tell him that I had had a bad dream. I didn't think I could tell him I was crying about Lonny. After two weeks, I again thought I was going crazy.

I was still working on the adolescent psych unit and asked the ward chief to give me the name of a psychiatrist I could talk to about my dreams. I saw Dr. G. weekly for about four months. On one occasion when I was crying my eyes out, Dr. G. interrupted me and asked if I could help him redecorate his office. I thought how insensitive he was. He then said that he wanted to put a pedestal in the office and where did I think it should be placed. Then it hit me what he was getting at.

He said, "Lonny was a God, wasn't he? So we'd better put him on a pedestal." In my grief I could only remember the good times. Dr. G. knew that I had to get angry.

My homework for that week was to come back and talk about the disagreements Lonny and I had had. That was very helpful, but the big break came on New Year's Eve.

I had told Dr. G. that the Christmas and New Year holidays were my roughest times. Dr. G. suggested that we meet at 4:00pm on New Year's Eve. I thought that was odd but went along with it.

When I walked into his office on New Year's Eve, he had rearranged the chairs. There were two chairs sitting across from each other and a third chair was far away from the other two. I immediately went toward the third chair but Dr. G. directed me to the chairs facing each other. I had to sit in one chair and pretend that Lonny was in the empty chair. I told him how devastated I was when he was killed and how my life was now. Then I switched chairs and listened as Lonny told Sue what to do with the rest of her life. I left feeling okay with a return visit scheduled for the next week.

The next time I saw Dr. G., I told him that I didn't need to see him again. He smiled and said, "I know. Isn't it wonderful?" As a psychiatric nurse, I had read about the empty chair technique but didn't realize how powerful it could be. The grief work I did with Dr. G. was one of the most important things I've ever done to help myself. I will forever be grateful to Dr. G.

Six years later, I was working at a local mental center. Dr. G. came to give us an in-service on transsexuals. We were sitting in a circle and as he talked he made eye contact with each of us. When he looked at me, he said "Sue, how are you doing?" I told him I was doing well and secretly I was pleased that he remembered me. After he left, a male peer asked me how I knew him. I said that I had done grief work with Dr. G. My peer suggested that I not tell people that I saw a psychiatrist. I was furious. I was not ashamed of the grief therapy I'd done and thought my peer was a hypocrite. As therapists, we were constantly telling our clients that seeking therapy was a positive choice. I have never been shy about telling people about the importance of grief therapy and feel that my experience has made me a much better grief therapist.

Ten years later, I was supervising two adult-inpatient psychiatric units and working with a young woman whose husband was killed in an oil rig explosion out in the ocean. She was suicidal and had taken an overdose of medication. She had two small children at home. She also had never seen his body and was having a difficult time accepting his death.

She was still suicidal when her psychiatrist told me that he was going to discharge her because he felt she didn't need to be hospitalized to do grief work. I asked him how many close relatives he had lost through death. He said none, that even his grandparents were still alive. I was amazed that he didn't know more about grief work and didn't realize that not seeing her husband's body made her grief more complicated. I tried to educate him, but I'm not sure he heard what I said.

When Lonny died, I stayed mad at God for a couple of years, but now I thank him for putting into my life the people who helped me during the worst experience of my life.

CHRISTMAS MEMORIES

At 10:45p.m. on Christmas Eve, I walked into the six-bed Intensive Care Unit. The lights were dimmed and the only sound was that of a respirator on the patient in Bed 1. Believe me, I was not prepared for the report I was about to receive from the harried evening nurse.

"I just want to give you the report and get out of here," she said as she nervously ran her hand through her hair. "There are only two patients tonight. In Bed 1 is Dr. Johnson. He had a stroke and is on a respirator. Oh, by the way, he's a V.I.P. He's one of the founding fathers of this hospital and is dearly loved by everyone. We're not doing much for him, just monitoring his vital signs, the respirator and giving him intravenous fluids. He hasn't responded at all since he had a stroke yesterday."

"In Bed 5 is a three-day-old baby, with a heart valve problem. She's the one that gave me fits all evening. When she reaches nine pounds, she will be transferred to Philadelphia for surgery, but she needs to gain weight first. I personally don't think she's going to make it. She stopped breathing thirteen times on my eight hour shift. I'm a nervous wreck. As you can see, she's in an oxygen tent and can't be taken out of it. Do you have any questions? If not, I'm out of here. This shift has been a nightmare." With that, she literally ran out of the unit.

The other person working with me was a nurse aide. She had worked permanent nights in the intensive care unit for six years and knew the respirator in and out. We made rounds to the bedside of each patient, and I told her I would take total responsibility for the baby if she helped me with the patient on the respirator.

Within fifteen minutes, the on-call resident and intern paid us a visit. They asked where I was from and about my nursing experience. One of them paled noticeably, and the other one grabbed a chair and sat down when I told them I was an adolescent psych nurse in a large university hospital in the mid west. They talked for about forty-five minutes and then after reviewing both patients' care with me, went off to bed. By then it was time for the baby girl's first feeding. There were signs all over her chart and on the oxygen tent not to take her out of the tent.

I warmed her bottle and proceeded to her crib with the oxygen tent. I put my arms through the sleeves of the tent and lifted her head to feed her. Now I knew why she kept choking and arresting on the evening shift. I laid her back down and went over to the nurse aide. "I want you to turn your back to Bed 5 and not look over there until I finish feeding her," I said. I felt if she didn't see me no one could fault her for what I was about to do next.

I re-warmed the bottle and returned to the baby's crib. I dragged a large rocking chair over and then bundled her up and took her out of the oxygen tent.

I held her close and talked to her in a soothing voice as I fed her three ounces of formula. I burped her between each ounce and then returned her to a sitting position in her oxygen tent. She went to sleep immediately. Two hours later, I fed her again in the same way. When I reviewed her chart, I found that in those two feedings she had taken more formula then she did on the entire evening shift.

Guess what? Right, she didn't choke, turn blue or stop breathing during any feeding all night long. I may not have been an intensive care nurse but I did realize the need for this newborn to be held close by another human being and not have her head jerked up and a bottle stuck in her mouth.

We made it through the night without any incidents. About 6:30a.m. the intern and resident were back with worried looks on their faces along with the head nurse. "Merry Christmas!" I said. "You may not want me to come back tonight when I tell you what I did with that sweet baby last night." I told them that I had taken her out of her oxygen tent to feed her. "If you don't want me to come back tonight, just call my parents' home and leave me a message."

I never received a call and returned Christmas night. You'll never guess what happened. All the signs to keep the baby in the oxygen tent to feed her were gone and replaced with signs saying to take her out to feed her.

I worked in the Intensive Care Unit again New Year's Eve and New Year's Night. Dr. Johnson was gone and the baby girl had been transferred to a hospital in Philadelphia. I can't remember much about those two nights, but on January 2nd the original intern and resident were back early in the morning. The resident said, "Sue, I don't know how you pulled off working in ICU being a psychiatric nurse, but you're a damned good nurse. If you ever want to come back to work here just give the hospital our names and we'll gladly give you a reference. You know, don't you, that neither of us slept much on Christmas Eve? We were sure you were going to hurt our patients."

Looking back all those years ago, I get scared. You see, my husband had been killed in Vietnam the previous January. In August, I'd taken a five and one-half month leave of absence from the adolescent unit and flown back home.

After a four month trip to Europe with two friends, I chose to spend the remaining time with my parents. I couldn't face the holidays and thought if I kept myself busy I wouldn't be so sad. I called the Osteopathic Hospital and volunteered to work Christmas Eve, Christmas night, New Year's Eve and New Year's night. The only unit that needed help was Intensive Care. So, after a two day orientation, I went to work. God was surely watching over me that time in my life because I was still in shock and not making good decisions for myself or for others. You can bet you wouldn't find me offering to work in an Intensive Care Unit today.

WHO'S STEALING THE NARCOTIC'S

"Sue, how can you just sit there and eat when Rachel needs her medication?" said the new nurse I was orientating. We were eating lunch at a long, brown table in the dining room of a local nursing home. I'd been on my feet since 7:00a.m., Rachel was sitting in her wheelchair in the doorway, staring at me. The glare she gave me could have melted ice. I told her that I had her shot ready and would bring it to her room in ten minutes when I finished my lunch.

Pat was our new nurse. She would take my place as the day charge nurse for two forty-bed units. I was going back to school to get my Bachelor's Degree and would be working from 3:00p.m. to 11:30p.m. on a different unit.

Rachel was forty-two years old and could not walk unassisted. She weighed eighty pounds and was so thin and emaciated that you would think she was at least sixty-five. Six years ago, Rachel had been hospitalized for pancreatitis. For pain she was given injectable Demerol. The infection went on so long and she was in so much pain, she became addicted to Demerol. On more than one occasion, Rachel tried to be withdrawn from the narcotic. However, the process became life threatening and so she remained addicted. Since Demerol pills had not been produced yet, she ended up living in a nursing home. What a tragedy! Her diagnosis and her doctors allowed her to become addicted and then couldn't reverse the process safely. By the time I met Rachel, she was so thin the only place to to give her an injection without hitting bone was in her thighs.

When I started working there, she was taking 50mg of Demerol every three hours. Within a year she was taking 50mg every two hours. I was assigned to another floor when I worked the evening shift but always knew what was happening in the lives of my original eighty patients. Within three months, Rachel needed 75mg of Demerol every two hours to ward off symptoms of withdrawal. A month later, she was taking 100 mg of Demerol every two hours. Her physician became quite suspicious and told the nursing director that someone was not giving Rachel her Demerol and probably taking it themselves.

An investigation ensued and sure enough someone was taking Rachel's Demerol herself, and injecting Rachel with sterile water. In a twenty-four hour time period, Rachel was only getting only two-thirds of her normal dose. That someone was Pat, the nurse who raised such a fuss with me when I had Rachel wait ten minutes for her shot.

Fourteen years later, I was the nursing supervisor for a twenty-four bed neuro-surgical unit in a large private hospital. One afternoon I received a phone call from an ER nurse who had been a patient on our unit. She told me that she was charged for twelve Percocet pills and that she was allergic to Percocet. My first response was that she should call the business office and inform them that she hadn't taken any Percocet while in the hospital.

She said, "Sue, you're not getting it. Someone is stealing Percocet and signing it out to different patients."

Needless to say, I felt rather stupid and spent one or two hours a day for the next several weeks reviewing the unit narcotic book and the narcotic sign out sheets in the pharmacy. It appeared that the same nurse was signing out each dose. Next, I started visiting each patient who had Percocet signed out to them and asked if they got relief from the pain medication. All of the Percocet was signed out during the night, and two out of every three patients I interviewed denied taking any medication for pain. Some nurse working nights was signing out the Percocet.

It was very difficult to believe that someone that I liked and trusted could be stealing drugs. I realized that the night charge nurse's name was being signed for Percocet. She was about six months pregnant so I was sure it wasn't her and that someone was setting her up. We'd had several discussions about how she had stopped smoking and drinking alcohol when she realized she was pregnant. I finally had to conclude that she really was the one signing out the Percocet. The next step was so very hard for me to take. I had to notify the State Board of Nursing and the local police department. The police came and gave her a citation to appear in court.

I then fired her on the spot and escorted her out of the hospital. I was not involved any further, but I'm sure she lost her Nurse's License, at least temporarily, if not permanently.

I know I did what needed to be done. I may have saved that nurse and her baby's life, but reporting a peer was very difficult. Nurses and other disciplines in the medical profession are at a much higher risk for prescription drug abuse because medications are so readily accessible.

FOUR EMPTY BEDS

Grant was a sixteen-year old student, Bob, a fifty-eight-year old physical education teacher, Dave, a fifty-four-year old pharmacist and Jose, a forty-eight-year old drifter. What do you think these four males have in common?

Today was my second day back at work. I had been gone for three weeks burying my husband who had been killed in Vietnam. As I rang the buzzer to be admitted to the adolescent psychiatric ward, the head nurse told me to wait, she'd be right out. When she came to the door, Dr. B. was with her. They slipped out of the door, closing it quickly. Simultaneously, they told me that I didn't need to work today. "Oh yes I do, I've been idle too long." I felt I needed to get back into my routine to keep myself together. They kept insisting that I take the day off and I kept insisting that I needed to work. I finally asked them what was going on and why they didn't want me on the ward.

Monday night, Grant had hung himself in the closet in his room. He and Sally had run away that morning. When they returned, Sally told him she was going to tell the staff that they had sex while on the run. There was no suicide note, so everyone presumed he was fearful of the consequences. Dr. B. and Holly were only trying to protect me by suggesting that I not work that day. I, on the other hand, could not see a relationship between the two deaths. I had only known Grant for one day. Looking back, I now know that I was in shock and therefore did not have a reaction like my co-workers. We had several meetings that day with the other residents and I just performed my duties by rote.

As Dave and his wife came down the long hall to our psychiatric unit, his wife hurried ahead, grabbed a staff member and pleaded with her to lock the ward door. Dave's wife had tricked him in order to get him to the hospital. They lived in a nearby state and she asked him to drive her to our hospital to visit a neighbor.

When he realized what she had done, he was furious. A pharmacist by trade, he had been self-medicating for years and not doing a very good job of it. He suffered from bipolar illness and was in the manic phase. Back home, he had been behaving in outlandish ways. We were all angry with his wife for tricking him. However, in hindsight, I realize she was afraid of him and worried about her safety and the safety of the patrons of his pharmacy.

His wife left shortly after getting Dave admitted. He continued to be angry but passively so. The medications he had been taking made him suspicious and mistrustful. He spent the entire day in his room and only responded to questions with a yes or no answer. Early that evening, the staff held a group session in the dayroom. They asked Dave to attend but he refused. The group began and a female staff member left to re-invite Dave. On the way to his room, the phone rang. She answered the phone and was still talking when the group ended.

Twenty minutes later when a male staff member checked on Dave, he was in the bathroom. A rap on the door got no answer. The staff member tried to open the door, but it was locked from the inside. He ran to the nurses' station for the key.

When he opened the door, Dave was hanging on the back of the door. He had hung himself with his belt. He was a large man and it took several staff members to get him down. The hospital emergency team was called, but it was too late to resuscitate him. When the police arrived, they were furious because Dave had been taken down from the door. His wife had not gotten home yet when we tried to notify her of his death. Certainly, we knew that Dave was angry, but on admission neither he nor his wife gave us any indication that he was suicidal.

Bob, a friendly man who liked to talk, was admitted to our unit for depression. He had diabetes mellitus and, as a result had neuropathy in his legs and feet. Being a physical education teacher, he spent most of his workday standing.

Standing and walking for long periods of time had become quite painful for him.

He had been on an antidepressant, which he thought was helpful. However, he had gotten heart damage from it, and had to discontinue taking it. During this hospitalization, we were trying to find another solution for his depression. Initially, Bob was very verbal about wanting to die. We even told his wife to remove the gun from the house and take it to a neighbor or a police station. As the days went by, he stopped talking about death and, when asked directly, denied being suicidal. Since medications were out, we encouraged him to consider electric shock for the depression. He was very resistant to that idea.

When the 4th of July came, Bob asked for a four-hour pass to be with his wife.

They were invited to a neighbor's house for a barbecue. Even though Bob was denying being suicidal, I evaluated him at length and had him sign a no-suicide contract with me. His wife arrived at 11:00a.m. to pick him up. We discussed the contract with her. She said she felt comfortable taking him home and that they would be at a neighbor's house most of that time. Bob walked out with the no-suicide contract in his shirt pocket right over his heart. We had a staff member call in sick for the evening shift so I agreed to stay and work a double shift.

Three o'clock came and went. Soon it was four o'clock, and Bob had not returned from his pass. I called his home and a man answered. I asked for Bob and the man on the other end of the line asked who I was. I told him I was from the hospital and explained that Bob was late coming back from his pass. The man identified himself as a police officer and said that Bob was being airlifted to a hospital as we spoke. He had shot himself in the head. Bob was dead on arrival at the hospital.

I called Bob's wife daily for four days and finally got her. When I told her how sorry I was, she said, "Bob's where he wanted to be now."

I asked her what happened. She said that after the barbecue she was home sitting at her desk paying bills and Bob walked in with a gun pointed at his head.

She said she took the gun from him, removed the bullets and laid the gun down.

Bob picked up the gun, walked back into the bedroom, and thirty seconds later he shot himself in the head. He had left one bullet laying on the bed.

I was overwhelmed with sadness, anger and guilt. I guess in the back of my mind I must have felt that Bob was still suicidal since I had him sign a no-suicide contract. I was also angry with his wife for not removing the gun from the house.

Bob was such a gentle man, and I had seen such good results from electric shock treatments that I felt he could have been helped. He didn't need to die.

I met Jose while working at a local mental health center. His daughter brought him in because he was "talking crazy." Laura didn't know her father well because he abandoned the family when she was just eight-years old. Just last week, he came back to town and looked up his long lost family.

Laura was married, with a family of her own, but she agreed to take Jose in.

They would make a bedroom for him in their basement. I met with Jose a total of three times. Two of those times were for medication evaluations with our staff psychiatrist. Jose spent the last twenty years in and out of prisons, detox-units and state mental hospitals. Yes, Jose had a mental illness, which he covered up by drinking. When he drank, he didn't hear voices.

Three weeks after I met him, Laura called me and said that her father was dead. She and her husband were out shopping for a bed for Jose while her eight-year old daughter was playing at the neighbor's house. The child ran home to get something and found her grandfather hanging by the rafters in the basement.

It was our policy at the mental health center to hold a psychological autopsy when a client committed suicide. Jose was Hispanic from "the old school." The morning of his death, while sitting in the back yard eating breakfast with his family, a butterfly landed on his arm. "That you, Ellie?" he said. Laura didn't know what he meant and just thought he was talking crazy again.

During our psychological autopsy, our *Curandera, a Mexican* medicine woman, interpreted his statement. Ellie had been Jose's girlfriend for the last ten years. The last time Jose was in detox, Ellie died during an asthma attack. Jose was distraught when he returned home and found out that Ellie was dead. That's why he came back to his home town. According to folklore, Jose thought that butterfly landing on his arm was Ellie telling him it was time for him to join her.

WHO KILLED MR. MYERS?

He was vague and mysterious when he called for an appointment at our Mental Health Center. After he answered all the intake questions with a simple yes or no, I made an appointment with him for the next morning.

Dan arrived on time dressed in blue jeans and a plaid flannel shirt. He was curt and seemed angry when I introduced myself to him. Because he was an inmate living in a halfway house on the grounds of the state hospital, he was required to receive mental health counseling. At the end of our first hour, I knew very little about him owing to his mistrust of "the system." However, over the next four months, I would learn much more than I wanted to know.

While in the state prison he had gotten a Bachelor's Degree in Psychology and he was furious that he hadn't been admitted as a special student to a Master's program at a large in-state university. He'd spent about five years behind bars before he convinced the parole board to allow him to live in a half-way house. The house rules were that he could leave as early as 6:00a.m. and he had to return by 8:00p.m. He also was required to have a job and pay room and board. Dan was employed by a local nursery.

Over the next four months, Dan told me he had been imprisoned along with two other men for the murder of Jake Myers, a sporting goods store owner. Dan and his two companions had broken into the sporting goods store late one night in June. Mr. Myers lived behind his store and heard them when they broke one of the gun cases. He confronted them with a loaded gun and told them to leave. Just before being confronted, they had loaded several revolvers. According to Dan, they told Mr. Myers to leave them alone because they would be leaving soon. Instead, one of them shot and killed him when he continued to point his gun at them.

As a human services professional, I could not believe my ears when Dan blamed Mr. Myers for his own death. He said, "It's the old man's own fault that he's dead. If he had just left us alone we wouldn't have had to shoot him."

As you might have imagined, there were times when I was afraid of him.

Consequently, I never saw Dan early in the morning or late at night when the two of us might be alone in the office. I always sat close to the door and let my co-workers know I was seeing Dan.

I was required to write quarterly reports to the parole board, and, from the very first session, I told Dan that my reports would contain what we talked about as well as his behavior during therapy. In my first report, I wrote that Dan said he continued to use marijuana and showed me clothing he bragged about shop lifting.

I also wrote that he continued to have trouble with his boss and peers on the job.

I didn't seal the letter because I knew Dan would read it and I didn't want my report to surprise him.

Dan didn't show up for his next two scheduled sessions and, during that two week period, I got a threatening phone call. I never received one before or after that time, so I assumed it was from Dan. The parole board did not grant him probation or allow him to move out of the halfway house. Since I did not hear from Dan for a month, I had to report that information to his parole officer.

Eight weeks later, Leon, one of my co-workers, told me that Dan had called him when he was on intakes demanding to change therapists. Leon told Dan that the three of us would have to meet together before he would agree to see him. I can't remember what happened at that meeting, but Leon took over as Dan's therapist, much to my relief.

About six months later, Leon came to our weekly meeting and reported that Dan had eloped from the halfway house and he was fearful that something would happen to him. Dan's body was found four weeks later. We never found out how he died, but, while Leon was sad, I personally was relieved. I guess to this day, I'm convinced that Dan was the one who shot Jake Myers, and he would hurt someone else if he wasn't incarcerated.

THEY JUST WANTED TO BE BLOOD BROTHERS

Sweat was running down my face and my hair had gone straight an hour ago.

I parked my small, foreign car at the curb. Leaving the windows down and the car unlocked, I climbed the steps at 101 E. State Street. On the loose floor-boards of the porch was a half-chewed welcome mat and a backless kitchen chair. As I rapped on the door, I heard a fierce growl.

The door was opened by a bald-headed man, wearing nothing but levis and holding a quart bottle of beer.

"Hi" I said, "My name is Sue, I'm a Public Health Nurse. City Memorial Hospital asked me to visit John Adams. Are you John?"

"Maybe, what do you need him for?"

"The nurses in the emergency room asked me to check on the cuts on his wrists to make sure he's okay."

'He thrust out his free hand and shook mine. "I'm Bob Adams, Johnny is my nephew. Come right in, missy, and I'll get Johnny for you."

Bob opened the door wide for me to enter. I had a hard time seeing because there were blankets covering both windows. Once my eyes adjusted, I saw in one corner the biggest, shiniest, Harley Davidson motorcycle I'd ever seen. There was an overstuffed chair with the springs coming right up through the center of the seat in another corner, and in yet another corner a black and tan German Shepherd with clumps of hair missing all over his back. The dog never took his eyes off of me.

The room smelled like old beer and cigarettes. On scattered orange crates were empty beer cans and ashtrays overflowing with cigarette butts. Empty vodka bottles turned over on the floor fought for space with the dust balls.

Removing a magazine, called "Biker" from the arm of the chair, Bob said, "Sit down, I'll get Johnny for you. He's in the bedroom with an Indian." I sat down gingerly on the overstuffed chair and got out my paperwork while Bob called Johnny.

Johnny came staggering into the room, pulling up his levis. When he saw me he yelled, "Jesus Christ, there really is someone out here."

"Hi, I'm Sue. The hospital asked me to stop by and see how your wrists are doing and make sure you don't have an infection. How did it happen anyway?"

"Biggest damn Indian I ever saw," he said. "He wanted to be my blood brother."

Laughingly, I said, "Right! Now tell me how it really happened?"

"I told you, he wanted to be my blood brother."

"Were you depressed? Were you trying to kill yourself?"

"No, I just wanted to be his blood brother."

"Bob, can you tell me how this happened?'

"Just like he said, biggest damned Indian you ever saw. He wanted to be our blood brother." With that, he thrust out both arms with identical cuts on both wrists.

As I looked at Bob's wrists, a middle-aged, Indian woman with eyes cast down hurried toward the front door.

"Come back tonight and bring your sister," Bob called after her.

I took one look at the two men and another at the German Shepherd and decided to get the heck out of there. I thrust a voucher at Johnny and asked him to sign it as proof that I had been there.

"If I don't sign this, then you can't leave, right?"

"Wrong," I yelled as I grabbed the voucher and my purse and ran out the door. I never looked back until I had locked my doors, wound up the windows and driven three blocks.

HE'S MINE?

I was greeted by five adults and one squealing baby on my first visit. Katie and her new-born son, Kirk, were referred to the visiting nurse service because of her mental illness.

Katie's mother graciously welcomed me and led me into the TV room. She introduced me to her husband, to Katie herself, to Katie's mother-in-law and, to "The Nurse," who was feeding a seven-day old baby. Katie was pacing around the room chain smoking and cussing.

I explained that the hospital requested that I visit Katie and Kirk to teach Katie about infant care, growth and development, and to be a resource person for her. Katie's mother-in-law and "The Nurse" were obviously skeptical; her parents looked relieved and Katie just kept pacing and cussing.

Katie had a chronic mental illness in the form of psychosis. Monthly, she received an intramuscular medication that practically rid her of all psychotic symptoms. She worked part-time at a local dress shop. During the third trimester of her pregnancy, she could no longer take the medication due to possible damage to her baby. As a result of being off of the medication, she was psychotic at the time of delivery.

That first day I visited Katie, she had no memory of delivering Kirk. She kept repeating, "He's not my kid. I can't stand that damned bawling all the time."

My job was to make an alliance with Katie so she would trust me enough to learn how to bond with Kirk and care for him. "The Nurse" lived in the home for about six weeks taking total care of Kirk. Whenever I observed an interaction between "The Nurse" and Katie, I noticed that she was very critical of Katie. On the delivery table, Katie was given her (IM) antipsychotic medication and she continued to receive it every month. Soon she was able to acknowledge Kirk as her child. However, during that time, Katie's mother-in-law had contacted Social Services, asking them to remove Kirk from the home of Katie and Mitch, the baby's father.

Mitch had always worked in his father's plumbing business and was extremely close to his parents until his mother called Social Services asking them to remove Kirk from his home. He took a stand and told his parents that Katie was his wife, and Kirk was his son, and they had to accept the situation or he would leave the family business. He continued to work with his father and his parents were less involved in his family's life.

After "The Nurse" departed, Katie's parents and Mitch took turns staying with Katie until she was able to be alone with Kirk. I continued to visit Katie and Kirk, weekly. Initially, Katie was timid and cautious around me, but as time went on, she became very interested in learning how to care for Kirk and loved him.

One day when Kirk was about eight-weeks old, I told Katie we were going to give Kirk a bath. I took the plastic baby tub into the bathroom and put it into the tub.

Bending over the tub, I turned on the water. Suddenly, I was soaking wet. Mitch had taken a shower that morning and left the lever in the shower position. Now I was getting my second shower of the day. I yelled for a towel and Katie started to cry. She was afraid that I was angry at her. I explained that it was my fault because I didn't check before turning on the water. There were about eight inches of snow on the ground that morning, so I borrowed her hair dryer to dry my hair and blouse before leaving.

As weeks turned into months, I realized that Katie had a wonderful sense of humor. Twice a year, I had to take my supervisor, Mary, on home visits so she could evaluate my interactions and skills. On that day, Katie and Kirk's house was my first visit. I introduced Katie to Mary and explained why Mary was with me.

Katie got a gleam in her eye and said "Did you tell Mary about the time you took a shower here?"

Mary's eyes got big and she said "A shower?" Katie started to giggle, as I stammered, trying to explain the incident to Mary.

Katie wasn't always that happy go lucky. One day when Kirk was about nine-months old, Katie opened the door and started to cry when she saw me. She told me that "The Nurse" had visited and told her that Kirk was retarded. She was crying like her heart was broken. I asked her why "The Nurse" said that. Katie said because Kirk wasn't crawling yet. We talked about how old Kirk was when she started to pay attention to him and care for him. I felt Kirk was at least two months behind simply because he had such a slow start. I told Katie that soon Kirk would start to crawl and catch up. Katie placed Kirk on the floor in a crawling position and I crawled toward him. He was a very alert and happy baby. Katie just needed to learn how to stimulate him. Katie always followed through with everything I taught her.

When I returned one month later, Katie greeted me with a big hug. "Guess what?" she said. "Kirk is now crawling and walking." I saw Katie, Kirk and Mitch only one more time and have wondered for years how they are and what they are doing now.

I did however run into Katie's Mother-in-law about ten years later at a Weight-Watchers meeting. She, the group leader, asked the new people to introduce themselves. When I said, "I'm Sue Tourtelot," she said, with a mean look on her face, "Yes, I know who you are." I never returned to her meeting.

DOES COWBOY STILL HUNT BUFFALO

After having been burglarized twice in two years, I decided to poll my neighbors in our Townhouse Corporation about a Neighborhood Watch Program.

I ventured out on a brisk, sunny afternoon in December. A dog barked when I rang the bell at the third house. A white-haired, elderly man opened the door a crack and asked me to "state my business." After my short explanation he invited me in. Once inside, he pulled the door closed and meticulously put on the chain lock. Seeing him do this I felt my heart start to pound so hard I thought it would jump out of my chest. Oh no, not again!

As a Public Health Nurse I had counseled many sex assault victims. On one occasion, I was seeing a young woman named Sara who had a sixteen-month old daughter. Sara and her boyfriend, Cowboy, had a party the weekend before. When they ran out of alcohol, Cowboy, his brother, and another male friend left to buy more booze. That left Sara, her baby, and Buffalo, Cowboy's best friend, alone in the apartment.

As soon as the other three men left, Buffalo grabbed the baby and said he was going to rape Sara. If she resisted, he would kill her daughter. Needless to say Sara put up no resistance. Buffalo left immediately following the rape.

Twenty minutes later, Cowboy, his brother, and friend returned to find Sara, half nude, lying on the couch crying. Her baby was patting her back. The very next Monday, I had a referral to visit Sara. I continued to visit her weekly to provide emotional support and assistance with any medical problems that might arise. The visits were going smoothly, Sara was having fewer nightmares, eating again and able to stay alone during the day when a fateful day arrived for me.

That morning, I called Sara and set up a visit for 2:00p.m. I arrived at 2:05p.m. and rang the doorbell to the security-locked building. When a man answered through the speaker, I said I was there to see Sara.

"What do you want with Sara?" the man said. As I started to answer, the apartment manager came through the locked door and told me to go on in. Sara had told her that I was coming today.

I walked up the stairs and rapped on Sara's apartment door. Cowboy opened the door and invited me to come in.

There was a second man standing behind the door who threw the deadbolt and slid the chain lock into place after I was inside. The apartment was dark. Loud music was playing and Sara was nowhere in sight. Facing both men squarely, I said, "Where's Sara?"

"Oh, she's in the shower," Cowboy said. I didn't hear any water running and the baby was gone. The hair stood up on the back of my neck as I thought, *WHAT'S HAPPENING HERE?* I was training to be a Women's Self Defense Instructor so I automatically dropped my purse and nurse's bag and assumed a defensive stance. I scanned the room and saw an open patio door.

Just then, the bathroom door opened and out walked Sara and her baby. I grabbed my purse and bag and suggested that we meet in her bedroom.

I cut that visit short. I couldn't wait to leave that apartment and relieve the fear that was overwhelming me.

"Well!" said my white haired neighbor, "Tell me about the Neighborhood Watch Program." I told him I'd been burglarized while at work and several other neighbors had reported break-ins to unattended cars and homes. I asked him to attend a planning meeting. Then I got up the nerve to ask him why he put the chain lock in place when I came in.

He started to smile and said, "Years ago my wife and I taught our dog how to open the front door with his front paws to let our cats out. My wife and cats are gone, but Rex here still opens the front door whenever he gets a chance." After laughing a little too much, I thanked my neighbor and left.

By the way, the last time I heard from Sara, Cowboy was still out hunting Buffalo.

NO FEELING

I knocked on the door to apartment 506. The occupant was a young man who needed his dressings changed. He was born with a condition in which he had no sense of sensation. His mother reported that as an infant he never wanted to be held and cuddled. In fact, he didn't want to be held at all. He would crawl under furniture and hide so no one could pick him up.

As a result of having no feeling, he would injure himself and not know he was hurt. Consequently, he would get major infections before getting treatment.

Eventually, he had both legs amputated above the knees due to gangrene. Presently, because he sat all the time, he had deep bed sores on both buttocks.

The door was unlocked, so when he yelled, "Come in," I entered the dark apartment. When I looked at him, he was holding a hand gun and was indicating with the gun where I should put my supplies. I got so angry that I walked right up to him and took the gun out of his hand. I walked across the room and laid it by the door. I thought I could get to the gun faster on my feet then he could on his hands.

With my hands on my hips, I walked back to him and stood right in front of him. I said, "If you ever have so much as a paring knife in your hands when a visiting nurse comes to see you, you will never see one of us again."

The reason I was visiting this young man was that he so intimidated his newly graduated, regular nurse, that she had come back to the office crying the day before. She was a young nurse with little experience in dealing with character disorders. He treated her like a batterer would treat his wife. You see, this young man was also a drug user and dealer. One never knew if he was using or how it might be affecting him.

Because his bed sores were so deep, we gave him an injection of a synthetic narcotic before changing his dressings. To this day, I'm not sure if he had pain or just liked the way the pain medication made him feel. He was very histrionic. He would go to the emergency room at University Hospital, and if he didn't get care right away, he would light himself on fire. That certainly got him immediate attention.

As I was opening the dressings I was going to use to pack his sores he said, "Give me the syringe and needle you used."

"No."

"Okay. I'll just shoot up with a dirty needle and if I get AIDS or Hepatitis, it's your fault."

"That's up to you," I said.

I completed the dressing change, and after reminding him that we would stop seeing him if he ever threatened a nurse again, I left.

Back at the office, I talked with his regular nurse. He had also threatened her with a gun. While she changed his dressings, he would berate her about what a lousy nurse she was. He demanded the syringes and needles from her and she gave them to him out of fear. Together, we went to talk with our supervisor and discussed whether our agency should continue to provide services to him in his home. The answer was no.

WHO'LL SEE DR. EDIE?

I had already made three home visits when I walked into the southeast visiting nurse office at 10:45a.m. All of the new referrals were taken except for one.

That one was for Dr. Edie Eberle. There were five nurses on our team, three public health nurses and two medical-surgical nurses. None of us would voluntarily visit a doctor or a nurse. I guess we were all intimidated by the mere title. Well, by coming late, I cooked my own goose. DR. EDIE was my new patient. Little did I know that I was the lucky one.

Dr. Edie lived six blocks from our office, which was a plus. She was terminally ill with pancreatic cancer. The chairman of the English department of a large state college, she was adored by her students. Both of her parents died of cancer at a young age. Edie told me that since she was over forty she thought that she was safe from getting cancer. She was diagnosed the end of August after a month of upper left-sided abdominal pain and died the day before Christmas.

Our local hospice would only accept patients who had a live-in family member to care for them. Since Edie lived alone, she was not eligible for hospice in-home care. However, when Edie chose not to live the remainder of her life in a hospital or hospice unit, her students stayed with her in her apartment day and night taking four and eight hour shifts.

In my varied nursing career, I had given palliative care to terminally ill patients, and I had counseled persons grieving the loss of a loved one or facing their own death. However, I had never given physical care and provided emotional care at the same time. Little did I know that Edie would become my teacher and mentor.

As I went through an extremely emotional time caring for a dying woman just four years my senior, I had no idea how that experience would shape my life.

Edie was such a warm, spiritual woman that I soon became very fond of her.

Often when I visited her she would cry and tell me of the reaction from her friends.

She'd say, "Sue, you're the only one I can talk to about dying other then my minister. When I try to tell my friends, they say, Edie don't worry, we'll get together in Europe next spring. They don't understand that I'll be dead by then."

Her mother had become addicted to drugs and Edie had bitter feelings towards her, and so she was extremely reluctant to take pain medication herself.

I would arrive for my daily visit and she would ask me to give her a long awaited back rub. I would plead with her to take some pain medication but she insisted, "I will not be like my mother." Her abdomen was getting bigger and harder by the day and still she would not accept pain medication.

I spent a lot of time with Edie, assessing the progression of her disease and administering physical care, but mostly I listened and learned from her. While I argued with God and questioned why He would take Edie from us, she accepted her impending death and thanked God for all his blessings. Dr. Edie had a strong faith.

She was sad that she was leaving her earthly life, but because of her deep faith she wasn't frightened. I will always remember Edie's courage and love for God. My minister always said, "Things don't happen by accident." God put Edie in my life so that she could be an example to me and so that I could learn from her. Edie went into the hospital twenty-four hours before she died. It was Dr. Edie's students who taught me what true Christianity is all about. They put their words into actions and honored Edie's wishes.

HOLIDAY TEA

While working for the local visiting nurse association, I was chosen to visit Molly Sue, because of my extensive psychiatric nursing background.

It was the week before Christmas and time for Molly Sue's biweekly Prolixin shot. On my last visit she gave me a Christmas card, so I decided to give her a religious bookmark and some holiday tea I'd made.

I rang the doorbell and stood there holding a glass jar of holiday tea decorated with a big red bow. Molly Sue came to the door and said, "What are you doing here?"

"Merry Christmas, Molly Sue. I'm here to give you your shot."

She looked at me, turned around, and ran into the kitchen. As I stood there with my face pressed against the screen door, I heard her mother shout, "Molly Sue, put down that knife. You're going to cut yourself."

Before I could move away from the door, it flew open and I was flat on my back, still holding the glass jar. Molly Sue was on top of me pulling my hair and hitting me in the face and head with a soup ladle. I was afraid the glass jar would break and one or both of us would get cut, so I continued to hold the jar between our bodies. I started yelling for Mrs. Fitzgerald, her mother, to get Molly Sue off of me. She was much smaller then Molly Sue. When she arrived, Molly Sue yelled at her to call the cops.

"Yes, please call the police," I said.

I was able to throw the jar onto the grass beside me, and with Mrs. Fitzgerald's help I got Molly Sue off of me. Molly Sue ran into the house to call the police and her mother ran after her. She stopped her from dialing 911, so she ran into her room.

Had the police arrived, I would have pressed charges against Molly Sue. I picked up the glass jar and headed back to my office. My supervisor called Mrs. Fitzgerald and told her I would no longer be giving Molly Sue her much needed intra-muscular medication.

Molly Sue had a chronic mental illness and one of the manifestations of her illness was paranoid behavior. She had numerous hospitalizations in her thirty-two years. At that time, there was a trend to keep psychiatric patients in the community rather then a hospital. So, Molly Sue was living at home with her mother and seeing a private psychiatrist on a monthly basis.

Molly Sue's father died of a heart attack four years earlier. Apparently, her father was more capable of dealing with her behavior then her mother and when he died she became more violent. The Fitzgerald home was a two-bedroom ranch with a kitchen, dining room, and one bathroom. Walking into the house was a bit scary since the drapes were drawn and there was only a narrow path to walk through the living room. Molly Sue and her mother lived in the kitchen and the two bed rooms. The living room and dining room were stacked from floor to ceiling with boxes.

The neighbors were so leery of the Fitzgeralds that they would not allow their children to play in their own unfenced yards or walk down the sidewalk in front of the Fitzgerald home. The parish priest had forbidden Mrs. Fitzgerald from bringing Molly Sue to mass because she upset the other parishioners too much. It seemed that every time Molly Sue entered the cathedral she lapped up all of the holy water.

After the Christmas incident, I was contacted by Molly Sue's psychiatrist.

He asked me to join him and Molly Sue at their next session. The topic was what happened the week before Christmas. I explained that since Molly Sue had given me a Christmas card, I wanted to reciprocate and give her a bookmark for her Bible, which she always read over and over, while I gave her the Prolixin injections.

I made a large batch of holiday tea and was giving a small amount to all of my clients. During the session, Molly Sue would not talk except to say that I was evil.

I never saw Molly Sue again after that day.

As the years have passed, I've spent a lot of time pondering that situation.

My only conclusion is that when Molly Sue saw the ribbon on the holiday tea and the wrapped bookmark, she felt she didn't deserve a gift and had to prove to me what a bad person she was. I certainly learned more from my experience with Molly Sue than from many of the other psychiatric patients I've worked with over the last thirty-five years.

HOW DID HE KNOW?

"How did he know?" She asked me within the first five minutes of my visit.

We were sitting in Katie's kitchen. She was chain smoking and couldn't sit still.

"How did he know what?"

"How did he know that I wore my skirts too short in junior high school and that my father told me that I was asking for trouble?"

I was working as a public health nurse for our local Visiting Nurse Service.

Katie had been raped on Saturday night and on Monday morning I was there to offer her support and information on any medical issues that could arise as a result of the rape.

Katie was twenty-seven years old and worked as a middle manager for a local department store. She loved to dance and because she was single, she went dancing every Saturday night with a married couple. After dancing, they would go to a twenty-four hour restaurant for an early breakfast. At midnight, the couple said they were ready to go eat. Katie said she still wanted to dance some more and she would meet them at the restaurant in forty-five minutes. She jumped into her older model, baby blue convertible and drove down the road to another bar.

As she pulled into a parking space close to the front door, a drunk staggered up to her car and said, "How much, baby?"

"More than you can afford!" She quipped as she got out of her car.

Suddenly, the drunk grabbed her and told her she was under arrest for solicitation. He pulled out a police badge and told her to get back into her car. She did as he ordered. He asked for her name, address and her driver's license. She was a law abiding citizen and cooperated fully with him. After getting her name and address, he pulled her out of the car and said, "You're coming with me." He dragged her into the bar, and calling the bartender by name, told him to keep an eye on her while he made a phone call.

When he returned, he told her he was taking her downtown. He said good night to the bartender and twisting her arm, dragged her back outside. He shoved her into the driver's side of the car and told her to move over, that he was driving.

Leaving the parking lot, he turned right instead of left towards the police station.

He drove to an empty field and told her that he had done her a favor and now she was going to do him one. He raped her all the while using his revolver to intimidate her. Afterwards, he drove her back to the bar, got out of the car and walked away.

In shock, she went straight home, showered and scrubbed her body until it was raw. She fell asleep immediately but was soon awakened by a nightmare. At daylight, she got out her bicycle and rode to a big city park. After riding fast and feeling exhausted she rested under a tree. It was there that a co-worker found her crying her eyes out.

After sharing what happened to her the night before, the co-worker convinced her to report the rape to the police. He took her to the city hospital for an exam and a police interview. She told the detective that the man who raped her showed her his police badge and revolver. He told her the rapist was probably just posing as a police officer. Because she had showered and scrubbed herself, the physician was unable to collect any evidence. As a result, the detective asked her to come to the police station and take a lie detector test. She did and passed the test.

It was Monday when Katie remembered that the bartender had called her assailant by name. She called the detective and asked him to go with her to talk to the bartender. Unfortunately, the bartender was off on Monday so the trip had to be deferred for twenty-four hours. I was concerned that whoever this man was, had her name, address and phone number and could come to her apartment at any time.

I suggested that she move in with a friend for a period of time. She said she wasn't going to let this man chase her out of her home.

The next day, Katie and the detective went back to the bar. Sure enough, the bartender remembered the situation and verified that the assailant was indeed an off-duty policeman who frequented the bar.

The policeman was brought to the police station, questioned, and asked to take a lie detector test. If he refused, he would be fired. He refused and was discharged from the police force. I became really concerned because this man could again pose as a police officer and unexpectedly be in her apartment one day when she came home from work. Katie still refused to move or stay with a friend.

I continued to counsel Katie over the next four or five months. Her original question, "How did he know?" was a classic reaction to a sexual assault.

In order to understand their abuse, victims look first at their own behavior and often blame themselves. Katie was NOT to blame. Obviously, her perpetrator felt he had picked a good victim but in Katie's case he was wrong. I didn't hear from Katie for about eight months and then one day she called.

"Sue, guess what the jerk has done now? Because he lost his job, he's suing me in a civil court for defamation of character. Can you believe his nerve?"

"Well, believe me, he's not going to win this one."

It was then that I knew that Katie was a survivor and that she was healing.

RON'S STORY

"Ron is going to act out in some way when he comes back from pass. I just don't know how. He was acting really nasty when he left. He wouldn't tell anyone where he was going or when he would be back." That was the report I gave to the evening supervisor that unforgettable day. I was the supervisor of two psychiatric units in a large private hospital. One unit was for the chronically mentally ill and the other for persons without a psychotic diagnosis.

According to his history, Ron had been the victim of the diagnosis "Munchausen By Proxy." Munchausen By Proxy is a syndrome whereby an adult either makes up an illness or exaggerates a child's symptoms of an illness for their own purposes. As a child, Ron's mother took him from doctor to doctor subjecting him to tests and treatments that he didn't really need and had no merit. As a result, Ron despised his mother and had no relationship with her in his adult years. I think his dislike for women carried over from that relationship.

A thirty-five year old engineer for a prestigious company, Ron had been hospitalized on our unit at least two other times for depression. He had a long time relationship with his psychiatrist who shared his first name. Having tried many different anti-depressants and psychotherapy, Ron had chosen a series of electric shock treatments during this hospitalization. In addition to his depression, he also had a diagnosis in the class of character disorders. He was a divorced father who physically abused his wife. He was extremely bright with poor social skills. During group therapy, he was arrogant, intimidating, sarcastic and a put down artist.

Taking responsibility for his actions was not part of his makeup. Electric shock treatments are usually given in a series of four or six. Because of the short term amnesia following a treatment, they are usually spread out over two or three weeks. These treatments are extremely helpful for certain types of depression and have even been successful in treating schizophrenics who cannot tolerate anti-psychotic medications. Ron was entering the last week of his treatments when this incident occurred.

It was a Tuesday, September twenty-third. I remember the date because it was my sister's birthday. Three of my friends and I were playing bridge when my beeper went off. "Oh no, something awful has happened," I told my friends. I called the hospital and was told that the evening supervisor needed to speak to me.

"Sue you need to come to the hospital right away. Ron returned from his pass with a 357 Magnum gun and held everyone at bay for forty minutes. The hostage situation is over but the unit is in chaos."

Ron had returned from pass at 6:30p.m. There were three staff and fourteen patients on the unit, some of whom had visitors. He walked slowly down the long hall, and, when he reached the nurses' station, raised the gun and ordered the staff to get into the nurses' station. One staff member had the presence of mind to yell for all the patients to get in their rooms and shut the door. Ron then proceeded to herd the one staff nurse and two psychiatric technicians from one side of the nurses' station to the other by pointing the gun at them. He apparently enjoyed the power that he got from that action. Someone pushed the panic button that warned the other unit that there was trouble. Two more staff arrived on the unit and were also herded into the nurses' station.

For some reason he singled out Linda, the evening charge nurse, and kept yelling directly at her. By now the police had been called and were at the doorway to the unit and on the stairwell outside the other end of the unit by the nurses' station. They felt it unsafe to storm the unit and just kept monitoring the situation.

Finally, Ron threw a note at Linda and kept yelling, "Read it, read it!"

Linda was crying and could hardly see through her tears but read the two page letter slowly. When she finished reading it, Ron brought down the gun that he had been waving around in the air and shot himself in the lower leg. As the gun came down, two male psych techs flashed back to Vietnam and dove under the desk in the nurses' station. The two nurses, Donna and Linda, started towards Ron because his leg was bleeding profusely.

"Get back, don't touch me," he yelled as he brought the gun up and pointed it at them. He continued to bleed until he got pale and sweaty and started to shake.

The two nurses continued to beg him to let them help him, and he continued to point the 357 Magnum at them. Finally, he had lost so much blood that his head slumped to his chest and the hand holding the gun went limp and fell to his side. Donna ran to Ron and took the gun out of his hand, yelling for someone to call the hospital emergency team. She attempted to stop the flow of blood by putting pressure on the femoral artery. The emergency team arrived and took Ron to the (ICU) Intensive Care Unit immediately.

When I arrived twenty minutes later, the police were interviewing the five staff members. Donna came over to me and while she was telling me what happened, I picked up the plastic bag with the 357 inside. One of the policemen yelled at me to put the gun down. Have you ever held a 357 magnum? It was so large and heavy that I had to use both hands to hold it. I met with the five staff members as a group and individually. I then met with the staff and the fourteen patients to explain to them what had just happened and reassure them about their safety.

Everything was happening so fast, that I soon found myself running down the hall beside the litter Ron was on, informing him that I was putting him on a seventy-two hour psychiatric hold due to his actions before going to surgery He was on his way to x-ray to make sure that he hadn't hit an artery in his leg. He had put the wrong sized bullets in the gun. Had he used the right bullets, he would no longer have a lower leg.

By the time Ron went to surgery, the police had left the unit and the remaining patients had gone to bed. The staff and I rehashed the incident one more time before I left the hospital It was well past midnight when I got home.

I returned to the hospital at 6:00a.m. We tried to reach Ron's psychiatrist for several hours right after the incident and had left several messages for him to call the hospital as soon as he got the message. All calls were to no avail. I called again at 7:00a.m., still with no luck. Ron was in the ICU. His kidneys were not putting out enough urine so he was getting (IV) intravenous fluids and had a foley catheter inserted. His wrists were in leather restraints because the physicians were afraid he would rip out the stitches in his leg and hemorrhage.

The unit was still in chaos. Dr. Reynolds, our ward chief, arrived earlier than usual and met with the day staff and me. It was decided that when Ron was discharged from ICU, he would not be permitted to return to our unit. I asked Dr. Reynolds to be present when Ron's psychiatrist arrived on the unit. He stayed until 9:30a.m. and then left to see a private patient at his office. Dr. Ron Steigel arrived at 1O:30a.m., he was informed that Ron was in the Intensive Care Unit.

The ICU staff called and asked me to come and talk with Dr. Steigel.

When I arrived I overheard Ron, the patient, saying, "Ron, get this IV and catheter out of me and the restraints off." Dr. Steigel immediately went to Ron's chart and wrote an order to discontinue IV'S, foley catheter and restraints. I followed Dr. Steigel to the nurses' station and when he told the nurse he had written orders, I told him that she couldn't follow those orders.

"Just who do you think you are?" he said.

"I'm the person who has been here most of the time since Ron returned from his pass. Have you talked to the ICU doctors? Ron is not putting out enough urine, and the surgeons are afraid he'll mess with the surgery site if the restraints are removed. I'd have an order to put the restraints back on before they can be taken off. Please come back to the psychiatric unit and talk with me."

I can't remember exactly what happened next, but the IV'S, foley catheter and restraints stayed in place. Dr. Steigel refused to talk with the unit staff and me but he did call and talk with Dr. Reynolds. Dr. Reynolds returned to the unit by noon and reported that Dr. Steigel had told him his patient said that the unit staff had over reacted. I was so angry. I think I asked everyone I saw for the next week if they owned a gun. My fantasy was to go to Dr. Steigel's office with an unloaded gun and hold him at bay for half an hour and see how he reacted.

The next two weeks were horrible. Everyone was suffering from Post Traumatic Stress Disorder, (PTSD), patients and staff alike. Dr. Steigel continued to refuse to talk with the unit staff. They were calling in sick on a daily basis. I felt like a spool with arms. Every time I walked on to the unit, it felt like someone grabbed me and spun me around. Trying to make sense of Ron's behavior, I asked almost all of our attending psychiatrists if the electric shock treatments could have in some way regressed him and lowered his inhibitions to make him act that way.

They all said no.

I met with my immediate supervisor and asked that the hospital press charges against Ron for threatening the staff and patients and holding them hostage.

The hospital refused to press charges, stating since he was a patient he could counter sue the hospital. I felt, with the support from several psychiatrists and Ron's character disorder, he needed to be held responsible for his actions. Knowing that it would put my job in jeopardy, I went to the police department with the intention of pressing charges against Ron myself. The police would not allow me to press charges because the note Linda read was seen as a suicide note.

Two weeks later, I asked a Vietnam veteran who had co-written a book on PTSD to come and talk to us about the disorder. During his talk I started to cry.

My husband had been killed in Vietnam, and all that happened in the last two weeks was too much for me. I couldn't stop crying. When the speaker finished talking, I told my charge nurses that I had to go home. I walked into my supervisor's office and told her I was leaving and didn't know when or if I would return. I cried the whole way home and then cried myself to sleep. Hours later, I woke up and started crying again. This went on for about three days. My supervisor or the director of nurses called me everyday to check on me. Finally, on the third day, I called my best friend and asked her to go to a movie with me. She said she'd go but only if I stopped crying. After the movie we had a long talk. I told her I felt like I was falling apart. She said, "Sue I think it's time for you to see a therapist, I know a social worker you could see." I went home and made an appointment for the next day.

I went back to work the following Monday, but continued to see the social worker for three weeks. When I told her I thought I no longer needed to see her, she agreed. She said, "Before you go, Sue, tell me what was the most helpful and what has changed."

I replied, "I realized that the situation was crazy and not me." Right then, I decided to really think about whether I could continue to work at that hospital.

Ron was discharged from ICU to his brother's care. His brother took him back to his home in another state. Things started to level off on the unit. One of the techs, a Vietnam veteran, went into treatment at a local vet counseling center. He was in treatment for one year. Linda never returned to psychiatric nursing and to my knowledge, has never returned to the nursing profession.

About nine months later, I was sitting in a physician's meeting when Dr. Thomas turned to me and said, "Guess who I saw today?" Right, it was Ron and he was back in town. I never told the nursing staff because I felt it would only bring back that awful day. However, a few months later, one of my charge nurses asked to talk to me in private. She had run into Ron in her local grocery store. I told her I knew he was back in town but felt it best not to tell anyone. She agreed.

Ron's behavior affected a lot of lives that day in September. I only pray that each one of those people has worked through and grown from that experience.

SINS OF THE FATHERS

"Dr. H., Nathan reminds me of Joey Miller," I said. "Remember Joey Miller? He was the kid who was on the adolescent psychiatric unit in the late 60's."

"Later, he broke into a female college dormitory raped, and killed a coed. I was just sick about that. We all knew he had sexual problems, but never in my wildest dreams did I think he would do that."

Joey was from a small town where his father held a prominent public office.

Because there was no psychiatric facility in that area, he was admitted to our big city hospital. At fifteen, Joey was a tall, handsome, well built boy. Talking to members of the opposite sex was difficult for him because he was so shy. He was admitted to our unit because he was fond of wearing his mother's nightgowns and underwear. I'm sure his parents felt that if this behavior became public knowledge, it would have an effect on his father's position in the community.

I became Joey's primary nurse, meaning that I would spend time talking to Joey and helping him work on his problems more than any other staff member. Nurses were not allowed to be part of family meetings at that time, so I would give information to his psychiatrist prior to family meetings. I remember role-playing with Joey around talking with girls and other social skills. Joey had two brothers, a nineteen-year-old and an eight-year-old. I was shocked when I saw his family for the first time. His father's lips were blue and he looked very frail.

Tom, the older brother, appeared to be a body builder. His t-shirt was so tight over his biceps that it looked like he had balloons under his sleeves. The youngest boy, Jimmy, was an active little boy, and Mrs. Miller was thin and pale.

Joey was hospitalized for about two months, with weekly family meetings.

By the time he was discharged, he appeared more comfortable with girls, but I'm not sure we had dealt much with his wearing his mother's underwear.

Three months later, Joey was back. This time he was caught stealing a brassiere and panties from a neighbor's clothesline. I kept feeling that Joey had a secret that he wouldn't talk about. I asked him repeatedly if there was something he felt he couldn't talk about. He would only say, "I can't talk about it." Finally, one day when we were discussing his upcoming court date, he said, "If I tell you, my family will fall apart and I'll end up raising Jimmy." All of a sudden, things fell into place for me. I remembered that Joey told me his mother had breast cancer and was recovering from a mastectomy. His father's blue lips possibly indicated heart problems. Suddenly, I was sure that his father also wore women's clothes at home.

I told his psychiatrist that I was sure the family secret was that the dad also wore female clothing and that the boys were having sexual identity problems. Tom was going overboard on the body building and Joey was wearing his mother's under clothes. She looked at me like I was crazy and wondered aloud how she would approach the subject in family meeting.

At the next family meeting, the psychiatrist asked both parents how they felt about Joey wearing his mother's underwear. Mr. Miller immediately said that it was no big deal, that all boys put on their mother's clothes at some time in their lives. Mrs. Miller said nothing. I can't remember what ever became of that issue. In my mind, I was sure Joey felt that if he told on his dad, his dad would die of a heart attack and it would be his fault. After all, his mother already had cancer.

Joey was discharged from the hospital to be followed in his community on an outpatient basis. That was the last time I saw or heard about Joey until I read in a newspaper article that he broke into a college dorm and murdered a coed.

Fifteen years later, I was working with Dr. H. again and our newest resident was thirteen-year old Nathan. He came to us because he was out of control in his mother's home. A week before admission, he had witnessed his friend raping a five-year old girl and had not intervened.

One day, Nathan's dormitory staff called and said that Nathan needed to see me. He told me that he thought he needed a circumcision. When I asked him if he had been circumcised at birth, he said he didn't know. Since there was no male present, I was not about to examine him and told him I would have his male supervisor talk with him. The very next day, he came to my office asking to have his hemorrhoids checked. I asked him what a hemorrhoid was and he said he didn't know. He said it hurt when he had a bowel movement. I told him I would arrange for him to sit in a hot tub of water twice a day to shrink the hemorrhoids. On the third day, my assistant, who had just graduated from college, was in the office when Nathan's staff member called. He told me that Nathan said he had a hernia. I looked at my assistant and said, "I'll bet you one hundred dollars that Nathan says his hernia is in his scrotum." Sure enough, when I asked Nathan to point to where the hernia was he pointed to his scrotal area. I looked at him and asked him if he realized that his complaints for the last three days were around his genital area. He just looked at me. I told him I didn't know what he wanted from me, and asked if he could put it into words? He said no.

That day I went to his team consisting of a psychologist, a psychiatrist, a teacher, and four counselors. I told them of my interactions with Nathan the last three mornings. I said, "I don't know what to do but somehow we need to deal with all the sexual issues Nathan is having." I left that problem with the clinical team.

Nathan stayed with us for about two years. During that time he grew about ten inches and gained about fifty pounds. At fifteen, he appeared older than his age because of his size. Since his parents were divorced, and his mother remarried and left town, we were working to reunite him with his father.

During that time, Nathan developed a crush on his teacher. After one family meeting he asked his father to follow her home. Fortunately, his father didn't follow her home and reported the request at their next family meeting.

Needless to say, his teacher was quite shaken. Around this same time, Nathan told a member of the clinical team that he had a dream about a female counselor. He said his peers and staff had gone camping and were staying in a cabin.

In the dream, one of his peers had killed the female counselor and they were hiding her under the water in the bathtub. He said they were taking turns having sex with her body, and when the male counselors and male supervisor found out they also had sex with her. Shortly after Nathan reported the dream, that female counselor asked to transfer to the health office and work in there with me.

We were all very uncomfortable around Nathan, and I was fearful that some day he would commit a sexual crime. Then Nathan, ran away and was never picked up by the police or social services.

The story doesn't end there. Six months later, Nathan's father was an inpatient on an adult psychiatric unit in a big city hospital. During that hospitalization, he met a young man named John. John had just lost his mother and lived alone in the family home. John was "slow" and had never worked outside of his home. His mother had always cared for him. After her death, John became very depressed and ended up in the hospital. According to newspaper reports, his neighbors checked on him to make sure he was okay. On one of his passes from the hospital, John told a neighbor that he met a man at the hospital who was going to come and live with him. The neighbors were concerned and went to the hospital to talk with John's psychiatrist. They asked if that man John met was dangerous or if he could be trusted. The doctor told them not to worry, that the arrangement would work out well for both men.

Not only did Nathan's father move in with John, he also brought along his anorexic girlfriend who was hospitalized with the two men. Shortly thereafter, Nathan also moved in and the nightmare began. Within weeks, John was dead.

When the neighbors had not seen John for a few days and they noticed that his car was gone, they called the police.

The police found John sitting in the living room with a plastic bag over his head. He had been hit in the head and died of a brain injury. Apparently, the trio then rented a rug shampooer to clean up the blood on the rug and washed down the walls. They got into John's car and left town. They were found one week later in San Francisco and were returned to the town where the crime took place.

According to the local news, Nathan's father took responsibility for murdering John, but I have my own theory about who killed John.

I have worked with troubled, abused and neglected adolescents for over thirty years. And yet I am shocked and overwhelmed on a daily basis at the atrocities committed against children and at the children's behavior as a result of the trauma they suffered.

EVENTUALLY YOU HAVE TO PAY THE PIPER

"The Intensive Care Unit is on the phone. They want to know if we're ready for the young man who took the overdose. He's medically cleared now."

Within minutes, Jon was wheeled down the hall to our psychiatric unit.

After reading Jon's history, all of my nursing staff refused to work with him. Jon worked as a cameraman for a local television station. His job took him to the other side of the state and that's where the incident happened. One night while driving around, Jon forced a local woman into his car. He drove her out into the country where he raped and beat her. He later said he thought about killing her but instead pushed her out of the car and drove away. The attack happened in a small town, and Jon was apprehended within a few hours.

At the trial, the judge told Jon that the community would not stand for his behavior and found him guilty of kidnapping and sexual assault. Today was the day Jon was to be sentenced, but instead he was in the hospital. He had driven up to the mountains on Saturday and taken an overdose. When he didn't return home by midnight, his wife went looking for him. Instinctively, when she couldn't find him in town, she headed for their spot in the mountains. He was unconscious when she found him. He was airlifted to our hospital.

Since all of the nursing staff refused to work with him and I was the supervisor, I was elected. Earlier in my career, I had counseled many sex assault victims from eleven to seventy-five years of age. Now I was forced to look at an assault from the perpetrator's point of view.

I met with Jon daily for thirty to forty-five minutes. I tried to keep an open mind, but I kept recalling the anguish and fear of all those women I had counseled.

I was relieved, when after three days, he was discharged from the hospital. Several of my staff members expressed anger at me for meeting with Jon. I thought, well that's the last time we'll see him, and I was glad.

I was so wrong. Three months later we got another call from the Intensive Care Unit about Jon. His sentencing had been rescheduled, and the day before the hearing he took a hand gun and shot off part of his right ear. Naturally, he couldn't go to the hearing. He had to have plastic surgery on his ear. This time Jon said that he attempted to shoot himself in the head and failed. In twenty-four hours, he was back on our unit and I had to work with him again.

One day, when we were in a conference room, Jon began to pace around the room, and then yelled, "That damned woman has ruined my life."

The hair stood up on the back of my neck, and, before I thought about it, I blurted out, "Let's talk about who ruined whose life. That woman is afraid to be alone. She can't sleep and she is probably afraid to go out at night."

He appeared to be astounded that I would say such a thing. After all, for Jon it was all about what was happening to him. Later that day, I overheard him talking to his plastic surgeon. He asked the surgeon to order a brain scan for him because he was sure he must have something wrong with his brain to have raped that woman. When the surgeon sat down and wrote the order for the brain scan, I told him that he had just been manipulated. He got furious with me and essentially told me to just get the brain scan ordered.

Jon's brain scan was normal. There was nothing that would suggest that his behavior was a result of brain dysfunction. Jon never took any responsibility for his actions. However, he continued to blame his victim.

Jon's wife was a mental health professional, and I was amazed that she continued to support him and try to bail him out. It was my understanding that when he left the hospital this time, he would go directly to jail in the county where he committed the crime. In actuality, when the surgeon discharged him, his wife came and took him home. That was the last time I saw Jon but not the last time I heard about him.

About eighteen months later I was working in a new setting and my assistant said, "I need to tell you about an article I read about a man who was in the hospital you worked in."

Before she finished the story, I called him by name. The article was written from an interview with Jon while he was an inmate in the state penitentiary. The article was not accurate at all. None of the facts in his medical records were in the article. Instead, it was written in such a way that Jon sounded like the victim. I was furious that the reporter didn't get all the facts, only Jon's side of the story.

BABIES HAVING BABIES

It was my last night as a student nurse on the Labor and Delivery deck. Our rotation was only four weeks long, and so far I'd been present for two deliveries.

Husbands were not allowed in the delivery room during that era. I had hoped to take part in a natural child birth, but so far I had only been bitten, pinched and sworn at. Needless to say, I was really disappointed. When I walked in, I was told that we only had one woman in labor. This was her first pregnancy and she'd been in labor for twelve hours. Her husband was an elementary school teacher and she was twenty-two years old.

Three hours later Molly's labor was progressing and she was really uncomfortable. As she got closer to delivery, she let it slip that she was only sixteen-years old. She was so scared that she cried and screamed with each contraction. By the time she actually delivered her little boy, she admitted that she was only thirteen-years old and her husband was her sixth grade teacher. I couldn't believe it and couldn't wait to see this monster. I felt so sorry for her. Where were her parents?

What parents would allow their thirteen-year old daughter to marry a twenty eight-year old man? My shift was over before she delivered her baby.

Molly had a beautiful six-pound boy. Next, I went to the Post-Delivery unit.

At that time mothers and their babies stayed in the hospital for up to five days. We tried to teach Molly all that we could in those five days. I was heartbroken when I realized that she was unable to figure out how to increase the amount of powdered milk for his formula as he grew. Who would make this child's formula? Who would stimulate this baby?

The day before discharge, her husband brought in clothes for her to wear home. She was crying when I walked into her room the next morning.

She could not fit into the tight, black, skirt that he brought her to wear home. Apparently, he had told her if she wasn't able to fit into it, she was in real trouble. We scrambled around and finally put her into two hospital gowns. One was tied in the front and one tied in the back. Her husband arrived wearing knee-length, argyle socks, bermuda shorts and a beret. He checked her out of the hospital and left to get the car.

We bundled up the baby and went out the front door. In the driveway was her husband, sitting in a Volkswagen Beetle convertible with the top down. That was the last straw. The Nursing Director of Labor and Delivery, a tall, heavy woman, grabbed the baby out of my arms and marched up to the car to confront Molly's husband. Molly and her husband were from a neighboring state, and it would take them about two hours to get home. The director demanded that he put the top up on the car. He said no and she turned and started walking towards the hospital with his baby. The father relented and put up the top. Molly got into the car and was handed her baby boy. She was crying again, and so was everyone watching them drive away. I've often wondered in the last fifty years what happened to Molly and her beautiful baby boy.

Thirty-eight years later, while working in a sixty-eight bed treatment center for emotionally disturbed adolescents, I met Carrie and Tashia. Both girls were fourteen-years old and residents of the same unit. One day, I was asked to do a pregnancy test on both girls. Tashia and Carrie were both pregnant. In addition to the problems that brought them to our center, they now had bigger ones.

During family therapy the next week, Carrie and her mother decided to take two weeks to look at the pros and cons of Carrie having a baby. Eventually, Carrie and her mother chose to end the pregnancy through abortion. The decision was not made lightly. Carrie was scared and very sad. She had the procedure and then stayed home with her mother for several days before returning to our treatment center.

Tashia's mother blew up when she found out she was pregnant. She kept yelling that Tashia was going to have an abortion. If she refused, her mother said she could never come home again. She said she had raised her children and was not about to raise her daughter's baby. Certainly, all of the staff felt that Tashia should not have the baby and keep it. Tashia was prone to temper tantrums and when she didn't get her way she would throw herself on the floor and scream. We felt that without words we were giving Tashia our opinion. Therefore, we arranged for Tashia to have counseling from an outside source to look at all of her options. In the end, she decided to have an abortion for fear of being abandoned by her mother.

After the abortion, Tashia's mother drove up to our treatment center and told her to get out. She abruptly drove away.

That brings us to a Friday afternoon in July. It was 4:00p.m., and I was just leaving my office when Tashia's counselor called me on the phone. "Sue, you've got to come up here and see Tashia. She's writhing around on the couch, crying and holding her stomach. I think she may have a fever."

Her body temperature was 99.4 F. and her abdomen was so distended that she looked like she could be five months pregnant. After a complete assessment, I realized that Tashia was impacted with stool. She had not had a bowel movement in over three weeks. She was at great risk of having a paralytic ileus and needing to have the impaction surgically removed if we didn't do something quickly. The first thing I did was tell her to get off the couch and ride the exercise bike to get her peristalsis going. Her counselors thought I was being mean. They didn't understand the seriousness of the situation.

Tashia had been sexually abused at a very young age. Each time she got her period and cramps, she psychologically re-lived that abuse. When working with sexually abused children, there is an unspoken rule that you never give them an enema or even a suppository.

Since Tashia wanted to be pregnant so badly, she unconsciously stopped having bowel movements in order to look like she was still pregnant. In view of her previous abuse, I conferred with her mother, gynecologist, psychologist and our medical director before treating the impaction. I found myself giving her enemas daily for the next three days and laxatives at night by mouth. It took about five days to get her gastro-intestinal tract back to normal.

Carrie was discharged about nine months later. She returned to visit us when she was eighteen with a one-month old baby boy. She had graduated from high school and had a job. Tashia stayed with us for another year and a half and got pregnant immediately after discharge.

Laura's story was the only one with a happy ending. When I arrived at the Cruz home, Laura, her baby, her sister Maria, and her parents were waiting for me.

Joey was just two-weeks old. Laura was a thirteen-year old middle school student.

Public Health Nurses received referrals from all the local hospitals to teach new mothers about child care and growth and development. A robust little boy, Joey grew by leaps and bounds.

During the two weeks before I arrived, the family had fallen into a comfortable routine. Laura continued to go to school each day while Maria, who worked from 4:00p.m. to 12:00a.m., cared for Joey. When Laura got home from school she cared for Joey until 6:00p.m. After dinner, Laura's parents took care of Joey, so that Laura could do her homework and attend school activities. At 10:00p.m., Laura took over again until she left for school the next morning. I followed Laura and Joey for about nine months. Except for frequent ear infections, Joey was a healthy, well-adjusted baby. Support from Laura's family made all the difference in the world.

WALKING THE DOGS

My husband Dave came home from working construction in Vail, Colorado with an adorable bundle of fur. Since he was a papered, Norwegian Elkhound, he certainly had to have a formal name. He became Brucester Olie McTourtelot.

Bruce, because my husband's best friend in the Navy was Bruce, who when he visited us was not enthralled to have a dog named after him. Olie, because he was a Norwegian Elkhound, and the Mc came from our neighbors, the McDonalds because he spent a lot of time at their house. He had a beautiful puppy face even at eight years of age.

Bruce and I were buddies. We ran three miles every morning and every evening. Before going for a run, Bruce had to "do his business" on our lawn and then off we would go. Bruce ran on the sidewalk, occasionally peeing on a neighbor's bush, with me running in the street beside him. He, of course, was faster than me, so he would sit at each corner and wait for me to tell him it was okay for him to cross the street.

One morning, an animal control officer sat in his truck and watched us for about two blocks. He got out of his truck and said, "Miss, would you please come over here?" I had to think fast. First, I thought about pretending I was deaf and keep running, but I knew he'd just follow us home. So, I bit the bullet and stopped to talk to him. I called Bruce over, and he sat right beside me.

"I'm going to give you a ticket for not having your dog under control."

I was so dumbfounded, I said, "I have great control of my dog who is better behaved than most kids."

"Yes, but you don't have him on a leash, and Denver has a leash law." He gave me a ticket, and as I shook it at him, I told him I'd see him in court because I had every intention of fighting it.

A week later, I went to court and met with a referee. I explained my situation and, although he understood my plight, he had to give me a fine. He cut the fine in half and told me, "One of our local newsmen has already paid over one-thousand dollars in fines. He and his wife lived across the street from a large city park. Every morning they would cross the street with their two dogs and run in the park. When they crossed back over the street, the dog catcher was waiting for them with a ticket.

Tasha, a female elkhound, was about four-years old when I adopted her.

She was pretty headstrong and not nearly as easy to train as Bruce. I ran with her on a leash once a day. Since I lived in a townhouse, with no fenced-in yard, I had to take her out each night before bed. We'd go out the front door, around the grassy knoll beside my house, and in the back door via the patio.

One night when we went out the front door, I saw a tall, heavy set man leaning against the townhouse directly across from me, about seventy-five feet away.

At first, I didn't think much about it, but when he was there every few nights I started to get nervous. One Saturday afternoon, when my mother-in-law and I were leaving my house, I saw the same man lying in the grassy knoll beside my house.

The next night he was leaning against the house again and started towards me. Tasha and I ran around the side of my house and down the alley between two more groupings of townhouses. I saw a neighbor's kitchen light on and ran up and banged on the sliding glass door. "Please call 911 for me. A man was watching me and is coming towards me."

The police took fifteen minutes to arrive and by then the man was gone.

I said, "A man has been standing across the way watching me as I go out the front door to walk my dog and then tonight he started towards me. He stands there quite often."

"Do you know his name or where he lives?"

"No."

"I can't do anything about this unless you can give us a name or address. If this happens again and you find out where he lives, call us back." And he left.

Well, I realized he had to live close by so I decided to do some detective work.

I realized that somehow I was signaling him. It must be when I turned out the light in my second floor TV room.

I called my next door neighbor, Bonnie, and told her what was happening.

I asked her to help me by going outside and standing behind the bush beside her front door and see which house he came out of. She agreed, so the next night I called her and told her to go outside. Then I turned out the TV room light, put a leash on Tasha and went out the front door. The man was standing across the way.

I pretended not to see him and took Tasha around the house and in the back door.

I called Bonnie and she told me which house he came out of.

The next day I called the home owners association. I said, "I need the name and phone number of the man who lives at 9290 E. Ohio Ave. because he is stalking me."

The man on the other end of the phone said, "I'll give him a call and tell him to call you. What's your phone number?"

"No, you don't get it, the policeman said that I need his name, address and phone number if I need to call them again. Please give me his name and phone number."

"Okay," and he gave me the man's name and phone number.

I decided to try to deal with the situation myself. I called the stalker and said, "I'm the woman with the dog that you are watching when I take her out at night and IT NEEDS TO STOP! I'd like to meet with you during daylight hours in the grassy area between our homes to get this taken care of." I had asked Bonnie and her husband to go with me.

"No way, lady, if I was after you, believe me, you wouldn't see me coming."

"I want you to know that my policeman friend, my neighbor and two other friends now have your name, address and phone number and if anything happens to me, the police will be at your door."

"My wife works for the government and this could jeopardize her job. I'll have her come see you when she gets home from work." And he hung up the phone.

At 7:30 p.m. that night, my door bell rang and there stood a small, thin woman and a child about four-years old. She introduced herself as his wife and I invited her in. By the smell of her breath, I could tell she had been drinking.

I told her, "Your husband has been stalking me at night when I take my dog, Tasha, outside to go to the bathroom."

"Oh no," she said. "He was hurt while working on the railroad, and he goes out jogging every night to get back in shape."

"Believe me, hiding behind that spruce tree across the way and watching me is not jogging. The other night he started coming towards me and I ran and called the police. I've already told your husband that my policeman friend, neighbor and two friends have your husband's name and address. This has got to stop, I will call the police the next time it happens."

Six weeks later, she and her daughter moved out. I continued my routine with Tasha, and never saw that man again. When I get scared, I always have to take action to calm myself down, and that's what I did in this situation.

DR. B IS BACK

"Here he comes again!" Nurses who knew him in his prime might have described him as a "dandy." He was over six feet tall, with wide shoulders and a smile that could melt ice cubes. His wardrobe was the envy of other surgeons on the staff. He also didn't seem to have the personality of a surgeon. He was soft spoken and didn't throw instruments during surgery. I never heard him say a mean word to anyone.

That was ten years ago. Today, with his grey hair and a far away look in his eyes, you would not believe he was the same man. Dr. B was being admitted to the psychiatric unit for the third time to be withdrawn from Xanax, an anti-anxiety drug. He lost his license to practice medicine in this state, so had moved to a neighboring state and was still performing surgery. He continued to return to see his psychiatrist and be withdrawn in our state.

Xanax is prescribed for persons suffering from symptoms such as irritability, a smothering sensation, trouble getting to sleep and staying asleep, restlessness, difficulty concentrating, an exaggerated startle reflex, wringing of the hands and excessive worry about everyday problems. It is considered a class III drug, which according to the pharmacy board, means that it has therapeutic value but is not a drug that is abused.

I strongly disagree. I have seen many elderly clients who were prescribed Xanax for the anxiety they felt after a spouse's death. Initially, the medication helps them feel less anxious and able to concentrate better.

If you were to look up the adverse reactions to Xanax, you would find that they are irritability, insomnia, nervousness, memory impairment, tremor and dizziness. When these reactions occur, the patient usually thinks that the drug isn't working anymore and so they increase their dose. Soon, we see that person on our psychiatric unit so they can be safely withdrawn.

Withdrawing from Xanax can cause severe seizures. That is why Dr. B came into the hospital today.

A normal dose of Xanax might be 250mg two to four times a day or 500mg two times a day. The absolute maximum dose for adults is 1000mg a day. On admission, Dr. B was taking 16000mg a day. When he was performing a lengthy surgery, Dr. B would take 3000 to 4000mg before starting. Then he would have to stop halfway through and go out and take more Xanax because his hands were shaking so much he couldn't perform the intricate tasks required. We never got Dr. B down below 8000mg a day, on any of his admissions.

Eventually, Dr. B lost his license to practice medicine in any state. Then he lost his home, his wife, his family, and all his worldly possessions. One day, when his psychiatrist came to our unit, I asked him a question. How did Dr. B get so many Xanax at one time, and was he writing his own prescriptions? The astounding answer was no. The psychiatrist said he was prescribing the Xanax. I was so dumbfounded that I fell into a nearby chair.

"Why would you do that to him?" I asked. You won't believe his answer.

"Underneath all his charm, Dr. B is a very angry man. If he ever gets in touch with his anger he'll be lethal." I will never understand. I thought psychiatrists were supposed to help people deal with their emotions and not just medicate them.

Made in the USA
Coppell, TX
12 September 2023

21499998R00069